HIMALAYAN
SALT CRYSTAL LAMPS

For Healing, Harmony,
and Purification

CLÉMENCE LEFÈVRE

Translated by Judith Oringer

Healing Arts Press
Rochester, Vermont • Toronto, Canada

Healing Arts Press
One Park Street
Rochester, Vermont 05767
www.HealingArtsPress.com

Healing Arts Press is a division of Inner Traditions International

Copyright © 2003 by Éditions Exclusif
English translation © 2009 by Éditions Exclusif

Originally published in French under the title *Guide d'utilisation des lampes en crystal de sel* by Éditions Exclusif
First U.S. edition published in 2009 by Healing Arts Press

Note to the reader: This book is intended as an informational guide. The remedies, approaches, and techniques described herein are meant to supplement, and not to be a substitute for, professional medical care or treatment. They should not be used to treat a serious ailment without prior consultation with a qualified health care professional.

Library of Congress Cataloging-in-Publication Data
Lefèvre, Clémence.
  [Guide d'utilisation des lampes en crystal de sel. English]
  Himalayan salt crystal lamps for healing, harmony, and purification / Clémence Lefèvre ; translated by Judith Oringer. — 1st U.S. ed.
      p. cm.
  Summary: "The first practical book on how to use salt crystal lamps" —Provided by publisher.
  Includes index.
  ISBN 978-1-59477-309-9 (pbk.)
  1. Salt—Therapeutic use. 2. Salt—Psychic use. I. Title.
  RM666.S183L44 2009
  615.5—dc22

                                                    2009033072

Printed and bound in the United States by PA Hutchison

10 9 8 7 6 5 4

Text design by Jon Desautels and layout by Priscilla Baker
This book was typeset in Garamond Premier Pro with Arno Pro used as a display typeface

CONTENTS

INTRODUCTION

Imagine that you have in your possession a geological treasure that dates back millions of years—before mankind appeared—and holds the earth's secrets inside. Imagine that this jewel, which also holds the memory of the sea, is a tool for vitality and spiritual growth. This dream can now become reality thanks to salt crystal lamps, unique in their origin, age, and surprising powers of harmonization and revitalization.

Rock salt is found in deep deposits in many regions of the world, including France, Poland, and Persia to name just a few. It forms crystals when it is pressurized deep inside the earth. The Himalayan mountains are home to particularly old and lovely varieties of salt crystal, which are becoming increasingly popular around the world for use as table salt and bath salts, in addition to the much-loved salt crystal lamps.

These blocks of rock salt crystal from deep in the Himalayan mountains have absorbed mineral elements that enrich them and give them their delicate tones. Unlike regular rock salt, which is extracted from industrial quarries that can reach over half a mile deep, Himalayan salt crystal is extracted by traditional methods that have been used for thousands of years.

So what is a salt crystal lamp? It is a block of crystallized salt that has been carved out from the inside, leaving a hole into which a 40-watt bulb has been inserted. All you have to do is plug it in—the way you do a bedside lamp—for it to give off its soft, calming light. This light aids relaxation and meditation and also helps energize your whole body. These specific effects owe little to mere chance, or to magic or religious powers; though salt crystal lamps display some astonishing qualities, they do so for perfectly concrete, well-identified reasons. Throughout this book we will see how and why salt crystal lamps work, so that everyone can profit from their beneficial effects.

You can say good-bye forever to stress, recurring migraines, feelings of tiredness, insomnia, excessive nervousness, and lack of concentration. Thanks to salt crystal lamps, your home will become a source of energy, dynamism, and vitality that will continuously regenerate you. This most amazing tool for protection and harmonization is a work of nature, and through it, the natural world will become the absolute symbol of well-being for you. Your vital energy will be fully expressed at last. You will wake up in great shape, wanting to take a bite out of life.

Rock salt's protective powers have been known since earliest antiquity. It has been used continuously—not by chance, but because every civilization has understood the secrets of

A salt lamp placed in the bedroom will give off a calming, soft light. Its ionizing action will induce a refreshing sleep.

salt. Occult masters of old have put it to the test, feng shui practitioners have employed it, and researchers today are rediscovering it as medicine for the home (geobiology) and for alternative therapies. The rejuvenative powers of rock salt find their most perfect, sophisticated expression in salt crystal lamps.

Today, people are continually bombarded by harmful positive ions, whether they realize it or not. These positive ions are generated by diverse factors, including subterranean sources, Hartmann networks, and the vast increase in electrical appliances and power lines. The harmful waves produced by these networks can alter our health and disturb our mental dynamism, although we may not be aware of it. Salt crystal lamps offer a practical, unambiguous solution to these problems.

The rock salt that makes up each of these lamps, which are unique in form and color, was formed two hundred million years ago. Each vein and marbled surface is a wonder of nature; the variegated beauty of these lamps is a profound benefit. When they are turned on, the lamps give out a soft light that attracts our eyes and calms our nervous systems. They are wonderful for relieving stress and are therefore ideal aids in meditation and relaxation practices.

Salt crystal lamps can be set up in your place of work, your bedroom, a meditation area, or a living room. Once they are in place, you will see conflicts disappear as if by enchantment. You will feel yourself filled with a wonderful serenity that will lead you to more often do the right thing at the right time.

1

SALT, SYMBOL OF ETERNITY

One of the reasons that the mineral kingdom is so fascinating to us is because its very essence speaks of permanence and continuity in our world of perpetual change. Minerals are the fixed elements in a volatile world. In its inert state, a mineral can last for millions of years without changing its appearance or being subject to erosion.

Salt in its mineral form is an integral part of life on Earth and has also played a vital role in human development. Now that we have access to many methods of food preservation, we often forget that the use of salt, or "white gold," marked a turning point in humanity's history that was as decisive as the discovery of fire. In particular, salt accelerated the process by which many nomadic peoples became sedentary, as it gave them the ability, for the first time, of keeping food from spoiling and consequently allowed them to build up reserves in anticipation of those periods when the hunting was poor.

From that point on, the separation generally made between nomadic hunters and sedentary farmers was no longer pertinent. Moreover, the discovery of salt's usefulness may even have led to the beginnings of capitalism, as it created the real possibility of accumulating resources. Certainly, it allowed people to plan for their survival on a long-term basis, which is the very foundation of all human societies, whatever type they may be.

As we shall see later on, salt became the axis for a new world that was structured around it. Its social importance can only be compared with the major role played by oil today. Interestingly, salt's commercial value wasn't the only thing that made it desirable. Although it was a precious asset negotiated at a top price, and an object of intense speculation, salt and other minerals were also vital to many spiritual explorations.

In the Chinese contemplative tradition, for instance, stones are thought of as sisters to trees, because their subtle, enclosed lives are a perfect complement to the expansive life of plants. In Western magical traditions, various minerals have different powers that can be called upon in spells and ceremonies. Stones are also fantastic transmitters and receptors of all kinds of waves and vibrations, a feature that makes them extremely valuable to psychic explorers looking to enhance telepathic phenomena, as well as to the high-tech industry.

The qualities inherent in individual stones are perceptible immediately to anybody who touches them. After a few minutes of physical contact, you can feel the specific energies of a particular stone; this may be more or less intense for different people, and for different stones. Many people, even those who don't consider themselves mystical or spiritual, will decorate nooks in their homes and gardens with stones, minerals, and crystals.

All minerals contain the principle of eternal life. When we recognize this, we understand why stones are such powerful symbols in our consciousness and in our material environment. Salt actually prevents microbial proliferation and drains bad secretions from our bodies. It belongs both to earth and sea but is like a mirror crystallized from divine worlds. Like fire, it is likely to burn whoever handles it carelessly.

From this perspective, even the headstone of a grave is

not the sign of death we tend to think it; instead, it is more like a life-stone, which transforms what is perishable into something imperishable. In the realm of mineral symbolism, rock salt takes on a very special power. It symbolizes eternity, purity, fraternity, and divine protection all at the same time.

On an astrological level, rock salt is connected to Saturn, as well as to Aquarius and Capricorn. Saturn is the emblem of time, which crystallizes wisdom like a salt. All salt in its mineral form is crystalline, with each tiny crystal formed in the shape of a cube. Today we know about crystal's fantastic ability to capture and restore information, on both scientific and mystical levels. This is undoubtedly one of the reasons for the unique place salt occupies in initiatory practices throughout the world.

Salt is also widely used in various forms of magic. According to notions of sympathetic magic, by which the physical properties of a plant or element are indicative of its magical uses, rock salt's ability to preserve and protect foodstuffs and to overcome decomposition mean that it will have purifying, protective effects for the human race when used in magic ceremonies and spells. It is customary for people to throw salt over their shoulders to protect themselves from demons. Moreover, it is not uncommon in occultism that the protective circle is traced with rock salt.

In spite of salt's well-known corrosive properties (for example, sentencing someone to work in the salt mines was often tantamount to condemning him to death), salt was never used in the context of destructive magic. All the rituals that use salt are rites of purification, protection, and creation. This may be due to the fact that salt was the only means of conservation we had for three thousand years! This unique role gave salt a sacred, untouchable status.

Salt also played a large role in the practices of alchemy, where it was no less crucial than the philosopher's stone, though perhaps not as well known. The philosopher's stone, envisioned by many as a pure gold and sought by amateur alchemists the world over, was always understood by professionals to be a symbol most of all: it is what we possess that is the brightest in us, the most remarkable.

The core of alchemy is about attaining *quintessence,* the essence or soul of the universe—not by being radically opposed to matter but by seeing through it. In this sense, a spiritual, metaphysical search cannot be separated from a material, physical one. So matter becomes the vehicle for transcendence instead of an obstacle to it. (Had this idea been clearly expressed, it might have been worth the one-way ticket to the funeral pyres that was the fate of many practitioners of this art.) The alchemists were thus not seeking material power but genuine spiritual knowledge. In seeking to penetrate the heart of matter, a practitioner would go off in search of his divine essence. His material experiments with transmutation of the elements would go hand in hand with a practitioner's own transformation.

The important thing was not for him to succeed in creating the famous "philosopher's stone" but everything he would have seen, understood, and felt by taking such a path. Mastering matter without having mastered oneself would have been considered a sign of failure.

One of the most delicate, subtle aspects of alchemical research was the work done with color. As matter moved from one level of being to another, the color of its material would also be transformed. With rock salt, we can see this process writ large: natural sea salt is totally white and was long ago nicknamed "white gold," which will tell us something about its value. White is the symbol of purity because it is an unwritten page on which everything is still becoming, as it was in the world before the Fall, before Adam and Eve were chased out of Eden. It's no accident that the Gospel of St. Matthew describes those who bear the word of Christ as "the salt of the earth."

Yet, in the process of transmuting itself into rock salt deep in the earth, salt takes on an orange-colored hue. This orange echoes the precious fire of knowledge and suggests to us that we, too, can be transformed by deep contemplation of this powerful "flame."

2

"WHITE GOLD'S" FABULOUS ERA

How did salt, which comes from the sea, become rock salt, a depository of Earth's telluric powers? To understand the answer to this question, we will have to go back several hundred million years to the Middle Triassic, the oldest period of what prehistorians call the Mesozoic era, which began around two hundred forty million years ago. Diplodocus, iguanodons, and other dinosaurs frolicked with complete freedom. (Although no matter what Steven Spielberg and Michael Crichton say, these creatures do not belong in any way to the Jurassic era!) The emergent lands were a real jungle, for tropical heat dominated the whole planet.

Land itself was actually rare at this time—most of the planet was an enormous ocean. For instance, the only terrestrial portions of France that existed at the time were the areas that correspond to present-day Brittany and the Massif Central (a mountain range in the middle of France). The giant chains of the Alps and the Pyrénées mountains hadn't yet seen the light of day; in fact, they wouldn't arrive for a couple of million years.

At some point, an extraordinary climatic upheaval changed everything. The large reptiles disappeared, and seawaters evaporated in many places. In the zones that the sea had deserted, the treasure hidden away in the hollow of the waves became abruptly apparent. It was then that rock salt began its slow morphogenesis. The tectonic plates began to differentiate and move around the vast oceans. Through the faults that were created by these seismic shifts, mineral, metallic elements became integrated into salt deposits. In this process, the immaculate white salt was modified toward the orange-colored hues that one finds in salt crystal lamps today. It is astonishing to realize that when you look at a salt crystal lamp, two hundred million years are gazing back at you. It's enough to give you vertigo. Knowing all of this, you will perhaps be able to see these objects as more than simple decorations.

Now let us jump forward a few million years, to the point where mankind appears. From the first eras when all food that was hunted or gathered needed to be consumed quickly before it spoiled, we move on to the refinements made possible by the discovery of fire. Fire not only changed the flavor of food, it also provided the first techniques of food preservation: smoking and curing made it possible to keep meat from spoiling for a longer period of time. But that's nothing compared to the changes that came about with the discovery of salt.

By the time of the Bronze Age, a thousand years B.C., techniques had been established for evaporating seawater to get the salt out of it. Almost as soon as food comes into contact with salt, a portion of its water drains out and germs are prevented from spreading. With this innovation, it became possible to keep food intact for a tremendously long period of time; salted meat or fish could be kept for years without any spoilage. Techniques for smoking and curing food with fire were also widely used, but they aren't as efficient. So it wasn't until the discovery of salt that people had, for the first time, a practical, unique method for maintaining foodstuffs in an edible state.

Today, we have a hard time appreciating the importance of this large-scale innovation. But it's important to realize that actual canned food didn't become possible until the process of sterilization was perfected by Nicolas Appert in the nineteenth century. Refrigeration as we know it would only appear during the twentieth century. Between the Bronze Age and the beginning of the nineteenth century—a span of almost three thousand years—salt and, to a lesser extent, fire, were the only means of keeping foodstuffs from going bad. From that point on, salt became a precious object and would be the subject of much speculation.

By a curious synchronicity it seems that salt's qualities of conservation were discovered by many different civilizations at around the same time, even by cultures that had no contact with each other. Salt was used in Sumer (southern Mesopotamia), the Roman world, India, ancient China, as well as in Egypt and pre-Columbian America. It's a surprising concomitance of activity. The discovery of salt mines brought salt's benefits even to landlocked cultures.

In Rome a precious substance called *garum* was developed as both a remedy and a seasoning. Garum was a liqueur obtained by soaking fish and plants in salt. The commercial value of rock salt is well illustrated by the fact that its Latin root *sal* is the origin of the word *salary*. In other words, salt became a means of exchange and a highly prized method of payment.

In fourteenth-century France, salt production was heavily taxed by a specific levy called the *gabelle*. The gabelle taxed 30 percent of salt's sales at the time but would grow until it reached 2,000 percent on the eve of the French Revolution! However, France's regions were not all taxed equally. So from one corner of France to another, the salt tax could vary in proportions of one to ten. This was a real windfall for smugglers, who would travel back and forth between regions, buying salt where its price was at its lowest and then reselling it where it was the most expensive.

In India oppressive salt taxes imposed by the British on the native populace caused such hardship that they became the focus of one of Ghandi's early protests. The salt *satyagrahas* (protests) eventually brought Ghandi and his hopes for Indian independence into discussion with the British leaders.

Of course, the salt trade and history continue into our era, but they no longer assume such spectacular forms. Whereas before the early nineteenth century no home existed that didn't have a salting tub, the appearance of new methods of conservation and the expansion of industrial society reduced salt to merely one commodity among others.

Knowing the vital role that rock salt has played in the

history of humanity gives depth to the fascination we unconsciously feel when we gaze at salt lamps. Let us not forget, though, that our history with salt is not without its dark side. Many people have suffered in salt mines with dried-out lungs and burned eyes so that their family or village might prosper in the rock salt trade. Slaves and common-law prisoners were often forced to work for the enrichment of others, and, as we discussed earlier, entire populations were brought to the brink of starvation with unfair salt taxes. In the present day, 99 percent of the extraction of rock salt is done mechanically. Among those who still use the manual methods, working conditions are much less painful and much safer than those that were ruthlessly imposed in the past.

3

NEGATIVE IONS

It is a much-discussed fact that salt crystal lamps diffuse negative ions into the atmosphere, which are particularly good for the human organism. But what exactly are negative ions? And why are they good for us?

Every atom of matter is generally divided into an equal number of protons, which have a positive electrical charge, and electrons, which have a negative electrical charge. While the protons stay where they are, it sometimes happens that the electrons get wanderlust and feel like roaming around. Frequently, an electron packs up and leaves its atom. It may wander around for a bit, then choose to settle down in another passing atom.

Once an electron leaves its atom or arrives in a new one, we're no longer talking of atoms but of ions. An atom becomes an ion when it ceases to have an even number of electrons and protons. The atom becomes a positive ion when an electron leaves, because the protons with their positive electrical charges are now in a majority. The atom becomes a negative ion if it has to add one more place setting: in other words, if a foreign electron becomes a squatter in the atom, then the negatively charged electrons are greater in quantity than the protons.

The idea that negative ions could have a positive impact on living organisms was the fruit of many chance observations as well as focused experiments. As early as the late eighteenth century, scientists noted that static electricity seemed to benefit plant growth, and this fact was the kernel of many experiments and inventions for the next hundred years. Then, in 1899, a pair of German physicists, Julius Elster and Hans Friedrich Geitel, established that these beneficial effects were caused by electrically charged particles called ions. Yet it wasn't until 1932 that an American researcher, Dr. Clarence Hansell, discovered that ions could also have an impact on a person's state of mind.

After that point, there were many projects and experiments designed by scientists and psychologists alike to evaluate the effects of negative ions on human physiology and behavior. Professor J. M. Olivereau noted increased aggressive and/or depressive behavior, in both people and animals, in environ-ments that had few negative ions. On the other hand, such behavior decreased markedly when large amounts of negative ions were diffused into a room. Other researchers have dem-onstrated that an environment rich in negative ions reinforces the body's vital processes, slowing down and even reversing health problems such as pain, depression, fatigue, headaches, and asthma. Professor Albert Krueger, of the University of California at Berkeley, proved that the negative ions produced

A waterfall is a true diffuser of negative ions. Like a salt lamp,
it recharges our energy and vitality.

by thunderstorms and waterfalls are what cause our positive emotional and physical responses to them.

In Salzburg, Austria, two scientists established an obvious link between certain winds charged with positive ions and aggressive, pathogenic behaviors. It is thought that an environment too rich in positive ions, and consequently poor in negative ions, causes a lot of tiredness, trouble concentrating, repeated migraine headaches, insomnia, continual irritation, and recurrent depressive states. Experiments done on animals have shown that an environment totally saturated with positive ions (and therefore totally lacking in negative ones) will disrupt an animal's immune system.

Salt crystal lamps generate a constant flow of negative ions, compensating for the general lack of them existing in our modern world.

Studies suggest that we would benefit most from an environment that has about 1,000 to 1,500 negative ions per cubic centimeter of air. By comparison, the air after a thunderstorm attains densities of 2,000 negative ions per cubic centimeter. Most of the time, however, in our built environments, we remain far from that ideal: in a small town we generally find about 250 negative ions per cubic centimeter, scarcely 50 in a big city.

Salt crystal lamps propagate negative ions in the atmosphere, which purify the surrounding air.

Indoor environments are even less healthful. In most homes we find scarcely 100 negative ions per cubic centimeter; we shall see why later on. The interior of most cars and trucks has only about 10 negative ions per cubic centimeter; no wonder long drives make us tired! The areas most saturated with negative ions are the less populated ones: there

The saturated air in big cities absorbs negative ions (leaving only about 50 per cubic centimeter) and gives way to positive ions, which are a source of our stress, tiredness, lack of vitality, and headaches.

are 1,500 negative ions per cubic centimeter in mountainous regions and in the heart of a pine forest, 1,000 in a countryside with a small population. These figures clearly show that the more a zone is subject to air pollution, the poorer the atmosphere is in negative ions. But as we shall see, other types of pollution also threaten us.

Salt crystal lamps make it possible to limit some of the disadvantages of urban life by counterbalancing the harmful effects. They are really a tool for protection, even if you exclude the field of magical experience from such a definition. However, salt lamps don't merely improve our air quality; they literally bombard our organism with negative ions, and thus function as very powerful energizers. In this sense they are similar to ocean waves, which create negative ions through the phenomenon of ebb and flow, or conifer forests, which generate negative ions in the rubbing together of their pine needles. In both cases, these natural forces de-saturate the atmosphere. That is why we regenerate ourselves in these environments, independently of the air quality.

A simple walk along the seashore will recharge your organism's trace elements, like the salt lamp does.

4

CHROMOTHERAPY

Chromotherapy, also called color therapy, is a method of healing that uses the energetics of color to reorganize and rebalance our emotions and our physical health. It is based on the notion that a specific energy emanates from every color. These individual energies can exalt us or contaminate us, heighten certain aspects of our sensibility, limit deficiencies or, on the contrary, even accelerate them. It was the pragmatic, systematic observation of such epiphenomena that led to the development of chromotherapy. Like the majority of natural medicines, color therapy can't claim to be a substitute for all forms of allopathic* treatment, but it often constitutes an indispensable complement, energizing our self-healing processes. In addition, chromotherapy sometimes produces tangible improvements in cases where

*Loosely applied to the general practice of medicine today.

standard medicine fails or provides only random results.

The specific color of a salt crystal lamp has a significant effect on its healing actions. The influence of colored vibrations on our moods and our health becomes more obvious when we discuss tonalities that are especially clear-cut—like black. For instance, one of my acquaintances, out of pure nonconformity and a desire to do things differently from everybody else, decided to paint his bedroom black. After he had done so, he noticed that he was frequently overcome by depressive states and even suicidal impulses, so, needless to say, he hurriedly repainted his room.

When we paint different rooms in different colors, we often unconsciously choose the colors best suited to the activity we have in mind for that room. A warm, exciting color would be unwelcome in a bedroom, for example, and would cause insomnia and disturbed thoughts. For similar reasons, bright colors are often welcome in our kitchens. In the same way, the colors we wear very often reflect our internal states.

Chromotherapy explains a lot about crystal lamps' tremendous breadth of activity. We have already said that each lamp is totally unique because of the individual mineral-bearing elements that have surreptitiously penetrated its molecules. It is the way these elements are distributed within the molecules of salt that determines their specific color. Two hundred million years were needed for such a metamorphosis to be brought about; that's substantial development time.

The quantities of metals and their nature vary from one lamp to another, but there is one invariable constant: the orange tone. Orange appears in its entire range, going from the palest to the brightest, crossing from yellows to reds. It is the proportion of these tones that defines the color you see in any individual lamp—light or dark orange, saffron or brick color—and all the nuances contained between these polarities.*

The color orange is associated with the element of fire in Western tradition and in the practice of feng shui. Unlike the hotter fire that emanates from the color red, orange is a fire that doesn't burn or destroy; instead, it spreads a gentle heat. It is a setting sun, an autumnal shade, a controlled blaze, a long-held passion. It is the tone of our vital bursts of energy. Orange enhances our concentration and our ability to come up with new ideas.

Associated with heat—don't we say that oranges, the

---

*Orange refers to the color range of the lamps *when they are lit*. Unlit, many will appear as shades of pink.

fruit, are "sun-kissed?"—and having a solar configuration, orange is active and dynamic. It is characterized by a calm assurance that enables us to go forward without being afraid of destiny's ambushes. This color unquestionably carries with it enthusiasm, an appetite for living, and attentive, avid curiosity about the world around us. It mixes harmoniously with proactive people who know how to take their destiny in hand, so they can fulfill their dreams here and now. Orange, the color of action, can facilitate a break with a fatalist vision of things, thereby helping us to recover our dignity as co-creators of the universe.

In the chakra system, orange is related to the second, or Svadhisthana, chakra. Although many people are skeptical of the chakra system because it cannot be "proven" in the purely scientific sense of the term, I believe that traditions which have persisted over centuries and even millennia are in fact based on solid foundations—the methodical observation of phenomena and causality. That is the case with the chakra system of ancient Hindu tradition. It is a system of energetic centers spread along the body, each of which has a specific function and identity. By reviving deficient chakras and rebalancing overactive ones, we enable energy to circulate freely within us once again, on both physical and spiritual levels.

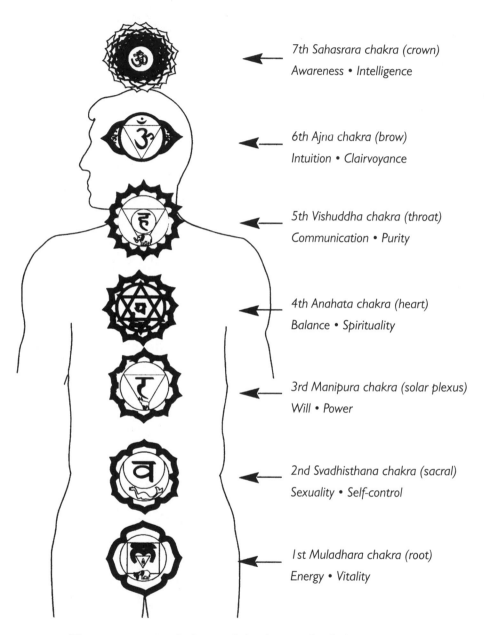

7th Sahasrara chakra (crown)
Awareness • Intelligence

6th Ajna chakra (brow)
Intuition • Clairvoyance

5th Vishuddha chakra (throat)
Communication • Purity

4th Anahata chakra (heart)
Balance • Spirituality

3rd Manipura chakra (solar plexus)
Will • Power

2nd Svadhisthana chakra (sacral)
Sexuality • Self-control

1st Muladhara chakra (root)
Energy • Vitality

The seven main chakras of the human body bear our
physical, psychic, and spiritual energy.

The Color Orange

Orange is the tone of the second chakra, Svadhisthana. The Svadhisthana center is located between the root chakra, which is associated with the color red, and the Manipura chakra, which is yellow. Between the chakras of red and yellow, the orange Svadhisthana chakra corresponds to people's genital zones and to the water element. (Remember that rock salt, too, is connected to the sea and therefore to water.) Svadhisthana governs the impulses connected to our animality—our sexuality and instinct—as well as the subconscious.

Representation of the Svadhisthana chakra, which acts on self-control and sexuality

From a chromotherapeutic point of view, the orange color has many applications. Sent out in the form of rays, this color makes it possible to do the following on a psychological level:

- Develop feelings of altruism and openness to others, to increase one's ability to feel empathy
- Awaken the joy of living and fight effectively against neurasthenia and depressive behavior
- Stimulate our courage in struggles and our ability to act effectively in ways that are less radical than those engendered by a red-colored wave
- Increase our clairvoyance, vigilance, and ability to have perspective on events
- Increase our personal magnetism, which gives us more influence over others
- Impart more assurance and self-control
- Make our minds more positive, in agreement with the fundamentals of dynamic psychology and creative optimism
- Strengthen courage and the determination to take our destiny in hand
- Halt impatience and angry impulses

- Calm down and channel people who are too quick-tempered
- Stimulate thinking and volitional faculties

On a physical level, the color orange acts to:

- Stimulate the libido
- Help regulate dysfunction in the menstrual cycle as well as in breast-feeding
- Strengthen the immune system
- Increase one's physical potential
- Energize the genital areas and enhance their function
- Ensure that the digestive system works well
- Fight bodily weakness and lack of appetite
- Calm down spasmodic and convulsive reactions
- Prevent pulmonary and circulatory deficiencies and accelerate the healing process in both these cases
- Support allopathic treatments for people who have asthma

In summary, we can state that one of the most obvious functions of the color orange is to regulate, channel, and magnify our energies, whether they are physical or mental. But orange is a cross between yellow and red, a blend that becomes more obvious as you observe the variation of colors in salt crystal lamps. The chromatic range that the orange color evolves through in these fantastic objects is absolutely inconceivable; it shows us nuances of color we have never seen before.

Some salt crystal lamps will oscillate more toward red, whereas others, in a pastel sparkle, will evoke more yellow. Every lamp doses its colors in a specific way, which affects its zones of influence. Of course, each one will have uniquely orange qualities, but it will also take on some vibratory particularities of red or yellow, according to whichever color it tends toward.

The Color Yellow

The initial association that the color yellow evokes in us is unquestionably the image of the sun. Although yellow often seems like a stimulating color, it actually belongs to the domain of colors that soothe more than they stimulate. This does not mean that yellow is enervating or anesthetizing; instead, it is a tone of real balance, especially for the neurological system. It is a color that acts powerfully on our neocortex and is associated with braininess, interior and spiritual life, and actions that are calmly thought out, rather than direct, rough intervention. For having stolen the powers of the sun—divine fire—Prometheus found himself chained to a rock, condemned to having his liver devoured eternally by an eagle.

In the Hindu tradition, yellow combines with the Manipura, or solar plexus, chakra—an essential emotional seat, as well as a key for mystical flight. Physically speaking, Manipura controls the liver and the stomach. It is no mere coincidence that the liver is associated with solar symbolism, or that this yellow chakra sits just above the energetic center that corresponds to the orange color. The Manipura chakra

Representation of the Manipura chakra, which acts
on power and will

also rules the astral body and offers us the possibility of traveling in the subtle worlds.

A color of peace and harmony, yellow is the sign of a fertile intellect. It supports mental faculties and the ability to think, as well as spiritual qualities leading toward evolution, inspiration, transcendence, and creativity.

According to chromotherapeutic principles, the yellow vibration makes it possible on a psychological level to:

- Limit the dispersion of our thoughts and put an end to our mind's confusion
- Develop an imaginary world and the creative aspect of our personality
- Greatly increase the intellect's performance and the ability to think and discern
- Increase our cerebral ability and memorization skills in the context of a test or competition
- Soothe people who have a hard time controlling their nerves and who are often victims of their "on-the-spot" emotive reactions
- Increase our aptitude for enthusiasm and happiness
- Acquire healthy ways of reasoning and an ability to gauge other people's qualities without judging them

- Increase our vigilance
- Relax the body and the mind

On a physical level, the color yellow enables us to:

- Regulate our vital energy more effectively
- Reduce the frequency and intensity of some migraine headaches (Don't forget, however, that these headaches are a symptom and that if you keep getting them, you should visit your doctor.)
- Strengthen the muscles and epidermis
- Relieve pain connected to liver or gallbladder problems
- Stimulate the pancreatic and intestinal systems (Lao-tzu said that the wise man was the one whose large intestine was functioning well.)
- Fight against all forms of digestive problems
- Ease suffering connected to curvatures of the spine
- Energize our neocortex and the little gray cells of our brains
- Accelerate the healing process of people suffering from diabetes

The Color Red

In the extreme richness of the tones between yellow and red, we have seen that there are, indeed, infinite variations of orange, some of which seem even to escape classification. So it can happen that an orange tends more toward red, in the way of a setting sun, for example. We are in the presence here of a shade of great ambiguity whose excess as well as lack can turn out to be dangerous. But don't worry: even if this color is always present in the suave glistening of salt crystal lamps, it is never in such a flagrant, dazzling way that it could become a destabilizing element. Salt lamps tend more toward pink, which has softer, more attenuated energies than red. Nevertheless, we owe it to ourselves to study all of this color's aspects.

The color red evokes blood more than anything else; indeed, the ambivalent nature of red is summed up perfectly by this dramatic symbol. Blood is the vital element, the flow of life that circulates within us and without which no existence would be possible. But it is also the expression of violence and aggressiveness. We refer to these aspects in popular parlance when we say of someone who has lost control of his impulses that "the blood went to his head" or "she saw red."

Red is something of a paradox, simultaneously a symbol of cruelty, dynamism, aggressiveness, courage, vital energy, and perversity. It is the link between Eros and Thanatos (Death).

The color of passionate love, exaggerated carnality, bodies on fire, feverish desire, and an aphrodisiac color if ever there was one, red can also be dangerous. Isn't the Master of Hell often depicted in red or purple clothing? Yet it is also the color worn by cardinals and popes. It seems that a certain degree of spiritual elevation is required for mastery of the powers inherent in the color red.

In Hindu tradition, the color red is associated with the Muladhara chakra, which sits below the orange Svadhisthana chakra. This energetic center is also called the root chakra, for it connects us to powerful Earth energies and anchors us in the material world. It is associated with the gallbladder and the element Earth, to which, as we have seen, rock salt is also attached.

The Muladhara chakra, which is located at the level of the sacrum, traditionally has considerable importance. That's where the infamous kundalini is coiled; the snake of brute, basic energy, whose rise through the chakras is synonymous with sacred ecstasy.

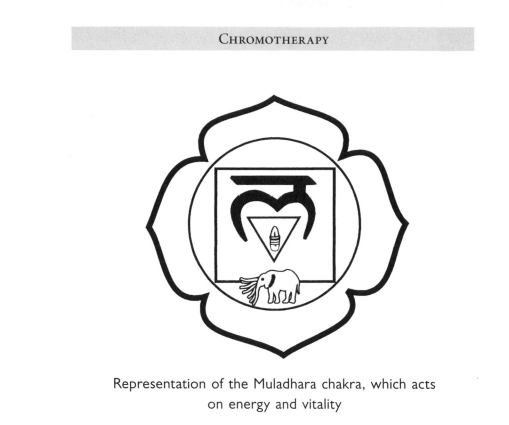

Representation of the Muladhara chakra, which acts
on energy and vitality

In chromotherapy, the red ray is used for the following psychological effects:

- To give you back a taste for fighting and going beyond your limits
- To impart energy to weary, depressed people
- To recover from a failure or depression
- To find the energy needed for action within yourself
- To spice up your love relationship

On a physical level, the color red is valued for its ability to:

- Increase your body's resistance and energize your immune system
- Improve muscle tone of the sexual organs
- Fight bulimia and anorexia—the red color is an important element of effective treatment for such cases
- Speed wound healing and the healing of eruptive diseases like chicken pox and measles
- Improve feelings of health in people suffering from pulmonary conditions
- Enhance blood circulation and harmonious breathing
- Relieve intestinal problems
- Act effectively on the nervous and lymphatic systems
- Limit the emergence of problems connected to cold weather and increase resistance to catching cold
- Remedy arterial or blood deficiencies
- Stimulate and energize the whole body

Now that you have a more detailed understanding of the power of the colors embodied in salt crystal lamps, you can use them more effectively. I highly recommend that you equip each room in your home with a salt crystal lamp, with an eye toward balancing and distributing the red and yellow tones to achieve a gentle orangey color. Alternatively, if you want to create a specific effect in a given room, you can install a lamp whose colors will best suit that need. In this sense, it is better not to place a reddish lamp in a bedroom, as it will be too overpowering. You can also move your lamps around to address specific temporary issues.

5

SALT CRYSTAL LAMPS IN THE HOME

One of the great scientific goals of the twentieth century was to separate knowledge from magic and superstition—to bring what was knowable into rational and quantifiable terms. Although there are areas where this attempt has unquestionably failed, there are others where it has progressed with giant leaps. Such is the case with what we today call geobiology, or medicine for the home.

Before building a home, ancient Romans typically let sheep graze on a terrain for a whole year. This would allow builders to see how the sheep reacted to the telluric vibrations (the vibrations coming from the earth) of the site. In the same way, many sacred buildings—from temples to churches and cathedrals—were purposely constructed on

Salt crystal lamps are an inexhaustible source of health
and harmony for the home.

grounds that had high telluric energies. In fact, many of these places have continued histories of religious monuments, with new construction often taking place at the exact site of earlier efforts.

From earliest antiquity, obvious links were drawn between states of consciousness, conditions of health, and the places where you lived and prayed. In the West this knowledge was swept under the carpet for centuries before it resurfaced in an astonishing way through the work of an exceptional individual. In the first half of the twentieth century, a French doctor, François Peyré, worried that certain places where people lived might be "cancerous houses." He noticed that nearly everyone who moved into these buildings would fall prey to serious pathologies. Other homes, while less extreme, also had many ill people living in them. For Doctor Peyré, the presence of subterranean water streams seemed to explain some of these cases, especially those homes that had been built on former marshes, but others did not answer to this criterion.

Peyré could not rest until he was able to formulate a coherent explanation. His theory of "Peyré radiation" posits that we are constantly being bombarded with two types of waves,

A pool of stagnant water near a house is a source of harmful waves. It makes the terrain humid and creates cavities and passages of subterranean water that are harmful for our health.

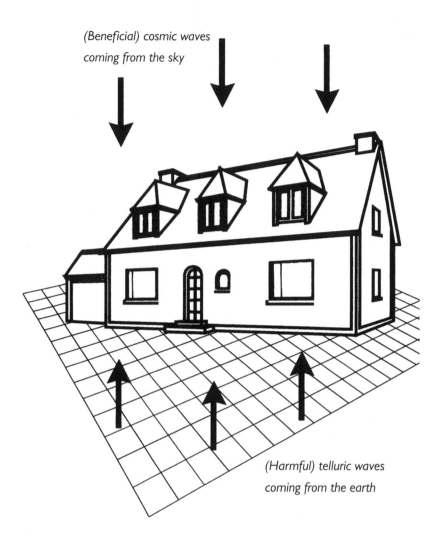

(Beneficial) cosmic waves coming from the sky

(Harmful) telluric waves coming from the earth

cosmic (coming from the sky) and telluric (from the depths of the earth). Whereas cosmic waves are beneficial to the human organism, telluric waves are often harmful (although they are very much appreciated by cats and ants). Under the earth, currents of telluric waves form vertical rectangles. Wherever two lines of telluric waves cross, human inhabitants will find their health and morale altered.

The diagram on page 46 illustrates Peyré's theory. The specific configuration of lines was verified by many experiments, as well as by case studies Peyré explored. But his theory was undoubtedly too innovative for the period. ("You are wrong," the writer Romain Rolland used to say, "when you are right too early.") He found no support in the scientific fraternity. In fact it would take several decades before another doctor, Ernst Hartmann, decided to continue his predecessor's work.

In Peyré's theory, Hartmann found a kind of echo of his own ideas, and he worked for years to verify their authenticity. He studied Peyré's files and also experimented in the field. The system of links drawn by Peyré seemed too timid to him. So he redrew the outlines under the name that we still use today: the Hartmann Network. During his lifetime, Hartmann continued to explore this new field of study, whose domain was the relationship between a living environment and its inhabitants. He created many instruments, including the infamous Hartmann wand, for measuring lines of energy, as well as stopgap measures for remedying the impact of harmful waves on human physiology and psychology.

Hartmann built the foundations of what would become a science within itself: geobiology, or medicine for the home. His successors have preserved and expanded upon his knowledge, and many important discoveries have been made in the past several decades. Much of this knowledge has already been integrated by researchers, architects, and builders. Some examples of this newer work include studies on the influence of specific shapes and materials used in construction and discoveries of harmful energies not categorized by Hartmann.

Foremost in this latter category are the electromagnetic waves emitted by most modern appliances. Even when they are not turned on, lamps, computers, television sets, microwaves, and other household appliances convey and magnify this kind of wave. This is a very disturbing fact, and one that is of enormous importance for people who live in houses located near high-tension lines.

A number of epidemiological surveys have noted that people in such houses suffer from many resistant kinds of insomnia, recurrent headaches, a noticeable decline in sexual desire, as well as from cardiovascular and blood-related problems. An overall weakening of the immune system has also been noticed.

Imagine what effect the proliferation of electromagnetic fields emitted by common objects may have on you. Their number is what makes them strong. Many apparatuses such as televisions and computers often remain in sleep mode—meaning they are still "on" and transmitting waves, even when they are not in use. Others—like cell phones, modems, and other "wireless" equipment—continue to diffuse an electromagnetic field through the atmosphere even when they're turned off. There is no place for us to hide, since we seem hooked on everything electric from music players to toothbrushes, not to mention cell phones, microwaves, and the like.

Returning to the Stone Age is out of the question of

A high-tension line near a house emits waves
(forms of micro-energy) that are extremely bad
for our physical and mental health.

course, but giving ourselves up to the damage is just as unthinkable, especially when simple, effective solutions do exist. The first solution has to do with a principle of precaution that we unfortunately don't think of very much: whenever you can, disconnect your appliances when you aren't using them. A dishwasher, electric stove, or washing machine doesn't need to be plugged in day and night, although it is hard to say the same about your refrigerator.

Another simple precaution is to stay some distance away from appliances when you use them. Microwaves, televisions, and CD players do not need close attention. People used to believe that television was only harmful if you sat

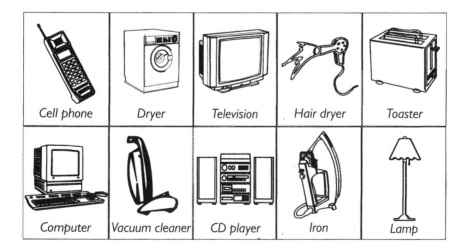

These everyday appliances emit electromagnetic waves
that are harmful to us.

too close to the screen while you watched it. Now it seems clear that you will be bombarded by a continuous electromagnetic flow whenever you're close to a television, whether you're actively watching it or not. This is extremely harmful to your health.

The third precaution turns out to be totally indispensable in light of what we have explored in this book: install a salt crystal lamp in every one of the rooms in your home. Choose different sizes and shades so that each one of them can find its place. As a general rule, the relative size of your lamp in a given space should be proportional to the time you spend in that room.

There are actually five distinct types of lamps. We say *types* and not *models* for the simple reason that every salt crystal lamp constitutes a unique and perfectly nonreproducible example. I can't insist enough on this point; no two lamps are the same. Salt crystal lamps are divided into types according to their weights, although these are understood within a range, rather than as precisely defined numbers.

The category of "mini" lamps generally describes salt blocks weighing less then four pounds, "small" lamps are usually between four and seven pounds, the "medium" bracket generally applies to lamps that are eight to twelve pounds, the "large" lamps thirteen to eighteen pounds, and finally, the "extra-large" lamps, which can weigh anything from eighteen pounds to thirty-five or more. Keep in mind, however, that different distributors may size their lamps differently; be sure to verify the size of a lamp before you purchase it.

In a small room, a bedroom for example, the smallest of the lamps should be sufficient. On the other hand, a large dining room should have a larger type. Know that these lamps never get saturated, whatever energies they may absorb. That goes for vibrational, metaphysical, and material charges. Not only will the negative ions bring a calming, regenerative atmosphere into each room of your house (and immediately soothe those most inclined to get irritated), but the salt crystal lamps will also absorb humidity. They also may help to kill airborne pathogens, keeping everyone in the household stronger and healthier.

From time to time you may notice liquid flowing from your lamp, or salt crystals accumulating around its base; these are evidence of the moisture it has absorbed and will clear up less than a half hour after you light it. Salt crystal lamps don't need specific maintenance—their antistatic qualities tend to prevent dirt and dust from settling on them. At most you can dust your lamp's surface with a soft, dry cloth. When you're not using your salt crystal lamps, they can be unplugged; even this way they will remain active and continue to diffuse an atmosphere of well-being and harmony. It is only when they are lit, however, that you can fully enjoy their shimmering colors and chromotherapeutic benefits.

Salt crystal lamps can stay lit for several hours. The negative ions they generate will in many ways counter the electromagnetic field they create. Moreover, the lamps will not get hot enough to burn you when you touch them, even after remaining lit for a relatively long period of time. Instead, they will give off gentle warmth and a fragrance midway between iodine and Jerusalem incense. It is a particularly pleasant smell that will excite your senses.

Kitchen

In the kitchen, a salt lamp will have a double effect, both soothing and energizing. It will stimulate your appetite, and will also have marvelous effects on your cooking skills! You will feel your kitchen to be a place of magic where you perform a kind of ritual, and you will spontaneously find the right ingredients and proportions to use in your cooking.

The food elements you use will be more charged with your positive feelings in this new space of peace, and your family and guests will respond to this, even if they don't know exactly how to express it.

Dining Room

In a dining room, the presence of a salt crystal lamp will make the conversations flow, even if the atmosphere has been relatively tense in the past. Whether you're feeding yourself, your family, or a number of guests, their digestion—like their appetites—will be effectively stimulated, and everyone will have increased pleasure in the food and in the conversation.

Living Room

In the living room, a large salt crystal lamp placed at the end of the room will clearly purify the atmosphere, both on the physical level as well as on subtle levels. Anyone entering this room will feel instantly at peace.

Office

Placing a salt crystal lamp in an office will prevent stress in the work environment and enable you to create a non-aggression zone around you. Your work will seem easier to perform, and your effectiveness will be greatly increased. Of course, depending on your profession and the attitudes of your superiors, it may be difficult to install a lamp in your workplace. In that case, you can reserve a room or the corner of a room in your home where you will meditate on work situations and resolve any issues that arise.

The salt lamp will quickly become an indispensable element in your living room, combining aesthetic comfort with a positive influence on your well-being.

Child's Bedroom

It is particularly advisable to put a salt crystal lamp of about four pounds in your child's bedroom, where it will quickly find its natural place. Your child's anxieties will be soothed, as will any tendencies toward insomnia, nightmares, and/or bedwetting. You can think of this lamp as your child's protector—a shield to keep his or her mind clearer, more serene, more balanced, and especially more self-confident. The lamp will also protect your child physically, as it will shelter him or her from a large number of illnesses.

A salt crystal lamp in your child's bedroom will create an environment of serenity and calm, soothing her nervousness and agitation. Insomnia and nightmares will quickly disappear.

Adult's Bedroom

In an adult's bedroom, a lamp can serve multiple functions. On one hand, it can actually help soothe nightmares or recurrent insomnia, as it does for children. For these purposes you would choose a lamp of a paler shade. On the other hand, if you wish to stimulate your libido and/or your spouse's, choose a lamp with a distinct, very assertive, lively orange color. It should be lit one or two hours before bedtime, but don't forget to turn it off when you have achieved your goal: otherwise, you run the risk of prolonging the initial state of excitement and having it turn into insomnia. Also remember that these remedies may not work immediately; be patient and wait a few days if the problem has existed for some time.

6

THE FENG SHUI OF SALT CRYSTAL LAMPS

Feng shui is an art of living that developed over a thousand years ago in China. Paradoxically, this ancient art from the East is adapting itself perfectly to our contemporary Western lives. Many people around the world are finding that feng shui can energize their daily existence by improving their health and their relationships with money, love, success, reputation, family, and friends.

Feng (wind)

Shui (water)

How does feng shui work? Quite simply by cultivating the circulation of harmonious, balanced energy in the places where we live and work. According to feng shui principles, the objects around us can either contribute to our balance or interfere with it: including the way objects are placed, the materials they're composed of, the direction they face, and their shape, color, and arrangement in a room can affect our physical and emotional energies.

This discipline relies on the notion that the condition of the rooms we inhabit reflects and reinforces our internal states. This is easily verifiable by experience. Haven't you ever felt the desire to rearrange your furniture, throw out certain objects, or acquire new ones simply because you were getting ready to change course in your life, or because your mental state was modified? You were no doubt doing feng shui without knowing it.

It was at the end of the 1960s that several feng shui masters who had emigrated to the United States decided to reveal the basic secrets of their art to a few special people. Little by little, this proof of the relationship between an individual and his or her daily environment spread like a powder trail. It reached its height thanks to Master Lin Yun, who was able to adapt these thousand-year-old methods to the urban environment starting in 1986. Since then, feng shui has continued to expand and has encountered growing enthusiasm.

The principles of feng shui are drawn from the Tao. According to the Tao, energy is meant to circulate freely; if it stagnates or rushes around too quickly, it will have negative effects on people, plants, and animals. If energy is circulating too much or too little inside a house or apartment, the occupants might be affected in many areas of their lives, from their physical health to the health of their marriage, their business, and their children.

In Taoist traditions, one of the primary ways to describe energy is in terms of its yin and yang manifestations. In this scheme, yin represents everything that is subdued, feminine, gentle, and interiorized: delicate curtains, shuttered lighting, or wicker furniture, for example. On the other hand, yang symbolizes what is bright, massive, and masculine—such as furniture made out of wood, or direct lighting. Balance between these two elements will be a permanent feature in healthy homes; excess or bad circulation of one or the other will lead to imbalances of energy that can be felt.

Another basic key to feng shui is the Five Element system, which gives us invaluable tools for evaluating and encouraging

CHART OF THE MAIN ATTRIBUTES
OF YIN AND YANG

Yin	Yang
Matter	Energy
Night	Day
Unconsciousness	Consciousness
Emotions	Logic
Intuition	Reason
Darkness	Light
Winter	Summer
Cold	Heat
Water	Fire
Woman	Man
Small	Large
Introversion	Extroversion
Land	Sky
Square	Circle
Moon	Sun
West	East
Space	Time
Death	Life

the harmony of a whole. The five elements in the Chinese tradition are Wood, Fire, Earth, Metal, and Water. Like yin and yang, these elements can be found in everyday objects in our homes—in the colors we see, the functions of particular appliances or furniture, and the composition of materials, among other things.

One simple way to determine which element a particular object belongs to is to go by its primary function. For example, houseplants, lawns, and trees are associated with the Wood element; their primary function is to grow. A stove, whether electric or microwave, should be placed under the heading of Fire, since its function is to heat things up. Chairs and tables and containers that hold things are associated with Earth. Electronics—with their mineral chips and wiring—belong to the Metal element, while sinks and tubs belong to the element Water.

The rule of thumb is very simple: the Five Elements should cohabit in good harmony with one another. In other words, the arrangement of your furniture and familiar objects should correspond to the mutually supportive relationships that are found between the elements in the natural world. These relationships are defined by the Creation cycle in Chinese philosophy.

CHART OF THE FIVE ELEMENTS AND
THEIR MAIN CORRESPONDENCES

	Wood	Fire	Earth	Metal	Water
Taste	Sour	Bitter	Sweet	Acrid	Salty
Season	Spring	Summer	Solstice/ Equinox	Autumn	Winter
Direction	East	South	Center	West	North
Activity	Birth	Growth	Transformation	Harvest	Storage
Weather	Wind	Heat	Humidity	Dryness	Rain/ Cold
Domestic animal	Lamb	Chicken	Cow	Dog	Pig
Note on the pentatonic scale	Kio	Tche	Xong	Chang	Yu
Organ	Gallbladder/ Liver	Heart	Spleen	Lungs	Kidneys
Color	Green	Red	Yellow	White	Black
Fluid	Tears	Sweat	Saliva	Nasal Mucus	Blood/ Urine
Affect/ Feeling/ Mood	Anger	Pleasure/ Laughter	Worry/ Obsession	Sadness/ Tears	Fear
Sense	Sight	Touch	Taste	Smell	Hearing

In the Creation cycle, each element is said to create the one that follows it. For example, water is vital for trees to grow (Water creates Wood), so we can therefore draw the conclusion that Water element and Wood element features go well together. In its turn, wood feeds fire, which regenerates the earth. Minerals such as iron and calcium, which are extracted from the earth, add nourishment to water, and then the cycle begins again.

In following this cycle, we see that the most beneficial combinations are Water-Wood, Wood-Fire, Fire-Earth, Earth-Metal, and Metal-Water. On the other hand, some combinations will diminish your vital potential and your ability to act effectively on all levels of your existence. These combinations are described by the Control cycle: Water puts out fire, which liquefies metal, which cuts wood. Wood (in the form of trees) absorbs the energy of the earth, which for its part dams water and prevents its flow. The combinations that are therefore strongly discouraged because of their ability to interfere with the harmonious circulation of *chi* (vital energy) include: Water-Fire, Fire-Metal, Metal-Wood, Wood-Earth, and Earth-Water.

There are simple ways to practice feng shui in your everyday life using these basic attributes. Let us suppose, for example, that you have an aquarium. Because an aquarium corresponds to the Water element, you would be wise to avoid placing Earth-element or Fire-element features too close to it—a chair, for instance, or a halogen lamp. You could harmonize these elements, however, if you were to insert the Wood element between them: Wood (a wooden table, for instance, or a healthy houseplant) would go well between Water and Earth, and between Water and Fire.

Similarly, separate sink (Water) and stove (Fire) by a wooden board and never leave cutting instruments (Metal) on a wooden base, for they will induce a notion of aggressiveness. Also, avoid putting metallic structures directly on wooden bookcases. It is interesting to note that many cultural traditions describe the same simple method for people to protect themselves against a spell: planting a knife or needle in the earth. Earth and Metal actually get along remarkably well.

Using these examples and the chart describing the affinities between the elements, you can already start arranging your home according to the principles of feng shui. There's no doubt you will feel much better.

With their gentle warmth and natural beauty, salt crystal lamps fit quite naturally within the practice of feng shui, and a growing number of practitioners recommend them. A central reason for their popularity among feng shui practitioners is that these fantastic objects actually manage to combine all the elements harmoniously! They create a complete Five Element cycle and can thereby correct deficiencies and excesses that may be present from other causes.

The oceanic origins of rock salt dictate its affiliation with the Water element; the environment through which it became transmuted and the quarries where it is mined connect it powerfully with the Earth. The mineral particles that infiltrate rock salt connect it to Metal, and Fire is transmitted to us through its rays of light as well as its orange-red color. You will notice that the one element missing from this lineup is Wood; now you understand why salt crystal lamps traditionally rest on wooden platforms.

To further invoke the complete cycle of the Five Elements, a lamp would ideally be placed on a transparent glass table, which would more strongly bring Water element's serenity into the room. A small, low table would take its place in the décor harmoniously. Remember that salt crystal lamps don't contradict and don't oppose any of the elements but on the contrary combine with each by completing its energy. That is why they easily have a place in the practice of feng shui.

7

RELAXATION TECHNIQUES WITH SALT CRYSTAL LAMPS

It's no secret that science and technology have developed considerably over the past several decades. But as we have seen, this progress hasn't come without side effects: in a world of constant growth, we are finding ourselves confronted with greater and greater pollution of all kinds. This pollution is not just in the air we breathe and the food and drink we absorb; we are bombarded by sound pollution, visual and light pollution, and a constant stream of microwaves, radiation, and electricity. In such an environment, our bodies stiffen against attacks. We live, think, feel, work, and love through these tensions and toxins. Our relationship with existence itself is altered by them.

Yet tension is sometimes necessary in life. It only becomes pathological when it's permanent. If we don't occasionally relieve our bodies and minds from these constant tensions, we will become more and more vulnerable to tiredness, nervous ailments, and more serious conditions. That is why relaxation is so vital: it offers increased awareness, which allows us to express our deepest selves. It is not just a passive state. By letting go of tight muscles and constricted thoughts, we move closer to the wholeness that all human beings seek.

Relaxation can be difficult to achieve, however. Most of us are easily upset by stressful thoughts, events, and physical challenges. Time-honored techniques of relaxation and meditation are helpful precisely because they take our minds and bodies out of the crush of everyday experience and bring us step-by-conscious-step into greater states of peace. They enable us to reestablish mind-body balance and let go of muscular and mental tensions. We return to a natural, instinctive state where we recover our energy and revitalize our nervous systems. Learning to become relaxed and mastering the art of unwinding will allow you to live your life in a healthy body, rid of all tensions and blockages. You will also learn to control your thoughts, your emotions, and your mental states.

In the following pages, you will find several variations of a basic relaxation technique that I have enjoyed for many years. It involves prompting yourself (in this case via an audio recording), to move mentally through your body and consciously relax its various parts. The fundamentals of this technique may already be familiar to you, since such "progressive relaxation" has become very well known in the past few decades.

When we let go of our muscles through relaxation techniques, our thoughts also slow down and release. We enter a deep hypnogogic state—a zone between waking and sleeping in which our brains emit alpha waves and we are deeply relaxed, yet aware of ourselves and our surroundings. By developing this special awareness, we have a formidable tool for personal power at our disposal. We can progressively replace attitudes of fear, being overemotional, and negativity with affirmations of strength and energy.

Ten to twenty minutes of deep relaxation per day, when enjoyed regularly, can enable us to get back into shape mentally and return to our joy in living. We can discover unknown potentials within ourselves and become physically and mentally younger and more vital.

Salt crystal lamps are a wonderful complement to deep

relaxation exercises. By closely combining the protective powers of salt, the qualities of chromotherapy, and the constant emission of negative ions, the lamps offer many advantages over other relaxation aids. For maximum benefit, your salt crystal lamp should be the only lighting in the room during your relaxation exercise. You should light it an hour or two before practicing.

One further unique benefit offered by salt crystal lamps is that you can touch them directly. During a sitting relaxation exercise or meditation practice, you can actually wrap your hands around the lamp, or you can lean your forehead lightly on the top of it. Its gentle glow will warm your skin without burning. If you are lying down, you can place the lamp so that it gently touches your hand, foot, or the top of your head.

You will gradually discover your own, very personal way of using salt lamps. If you enjoy touching the lamp during your practice, remember that the tiny salt particles penetrating your skin will be positive and regenerative. Whereas high doses of salt taken internally could wind up being harmful, even long-term exposure through your skin will be nourishing and beneficial. Furthermore, after you have left the salt lamp lit for an hour or two (the exact time-frame depends on its size and volume) you will notice that a subtle fragrance comes wafting from it. This aroma will enhance your relaxation techniques and meditation and may also have energetic benefits.

The relaxation method that follows has many uses and few contraindications. Simply choose the visualization that you

The salt lamp will serve as a support for meditation, enabling you to relax and recharge yourself thanks to its beneficial color and ionizing effect.

prefer. If you are afraid of water, for example, don't choose a visualization at the seashore. Opt instead for an image of the country, in a springtime landscape. And if for any reason you can't stand the color green, don't choose a field full of wild grass. The golden rule of this exercise is to please yourself.

Once you have mastered some simple relaxation techniques, you can teach them to your children. Regular relaxation exercises will be extremely helpful for children with emotional problems and those with difficulties at school. They are ready as soon as they are able to understand the instructions. Your child should participate in these efforts and feel a lot of satisfaction from them. If not, don't insist that she practice them; enhanced well-being cannot be forced. If you do practice with your child, use a small salt lamp, and don't place it in direct contact with his or her head. The exercise should be for a short duration and should be accompanied by light touches on the solar plexus and head.

Partners can also practice relaxation techniques together. This kind of shared practice is a wonderful antidote to the stresses and irritations we often share with our loved ones. Remember, however, not to force your partner to practice with you; relaxation is a choice.

Relaxation exercises and salt lamps are not taboo for

people suffering from cardiovascular problems or any other health issues. On the contrary, in some cases they can be helpful in making a real improvement. Older people will get a lot out of such exercises. They will see the pains of old age diminish and their mental faculties increase. When practiced regularly throughout our lives, relaxation techniques enable us to experience old age with grace and gratitude.

Relaxation techniques should be practiced in an isolated place. If need be, disconnect your phone and turn off your cell phone. The room should be lit only by one or two salt crystal lamps and must be absolutely sealed against drafts— don't hesitate to seal doors and windows that are badly adjusted. You should be stretched out on the floor with

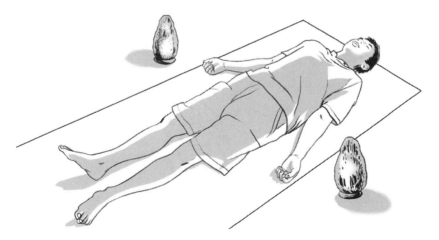

The combined effect of two lamps will be ideal for a deep, revitalizing relaxation session.

your eyes closed as you listen to a message that you have pre-recorded or that is being dictated by another person.

There are three degrees of relaxation practice:

- The basic relaxation technique (muscular)
- The deep relaxation technique (mental)
- Visualization

All of the relaxation techniques described in this chapter and their extensions—visualization exercises—will begin systematically with the "basic" relaxation that follows. It is better to master this basic technique perfectly before going on to more advanced exercises. You can obtain this mastery in a couple of days, if you feel strongly motivated, or else in a few months. It depends mainly on your personality and how regularly you practice. For most people, ten to twenty minutes a day will be ideal.

Use a gently persuasive voice to record the text that will serve you as a kind of spinal column for the relaxation exercise. Inhale between the lines and exhale as you say your text. Although this method may seem hard to you at first, you will easily take on the rhythm of speaking during exhalation. This will give more weight to your words. (Such a technique can be used whenever you want to convince someone you are talking to.) Take time to pause between every sentence. This time is needed to achieve bodily awareness.

The text below is a sample. You should record yourself or another person reading it, so you can follow along during your practice without having to read. You may choose to alter it slightly, but be sure to retain the basic sequence and style, reminding yourself of each body part and prompting yourself to relax it. Also, it is a good idea to practice a few times before making your recording, so that your finished product will be smooth and easy to follow without distraction.

Right now I am lying down and stretching out comfortably . . . my body is letting go and becoming heavier and heavier . . . I am becoming aware of my forehead . . . I am mentally erasing wrinkles of expression . . . the space between my eyebrows is relaxing, is letting go, is getting bigger . . . my eyelids are heavy . . . I am becoming aware of the tension behind my eyes, around my eyes, and I am letting it go . . . I am relaxing my jaw, my jaw muscles are loose . . . my tongue is flexible in my palate, my mouth is half open . . .

*I am relaxing the whole surface of my scalp . . .
I am relaxing the nape of my neck . . . and my neck
. . . I am letting my shoulders go . . . my arm muscles
are flexible like ivy . . . my elbows are relaxed . . .
my forearms . . . my wrists . . . the insides of my hands
. . . my fingers up to the fingertips and inward to the
bones . . .*

*I am thinking about my diaphragm . . . my dia-
phragm is dilated to enable my breath to circulate freely
. . . with ease . . . my belly is relaxing . . . I am loosen-
ing the ring around my abdomen . . . I am becoming
aware of my lower abdomen . . . of my sexual organs
. . . I am relaxing my perineum . . . the muscles of my
thighs are relaxed . . . my knees are perfectly lubricated
. . . my calves are flexible and light . . . my ankles . . .
my feet are letting go all the way up to my toes . . .*

*I am becoming aware of my back, which is relaxing,
whose whole length is stretching out along the floor . . .
I am letting go completely, perfectly . . . I am perfectly
relaxed . . . calm . . . peaceful . . . I am thinking about
my breathing, effortlessly . . . I am listening to it . . . I
am listening to myself breathe.*

At this point you can end this exercise, or you can go directly into a visualization for a specific condition. If you are ready to end the exercise, you will finish it off by gradually coming back to outside reality.

Right now, I am becoming gradually aware again of the outside world surrounding me . . . every new relaxation process will be deeper and more beneficial . . . I am taking three big breaths . . . I am gently stretching out my limbs . . . I am moving my toes . . . Radiating with life, I am opening my eyes.

For those who have not experienced this kind of guided meditation before, you will be interested to learn that each movement and attitude expressed on the tape will be reproduced naturally by you at the moment you hear it. So you will be doing more than just "listening" to the tape; you will be effortlessly following along with it. The many benefits of this simple exercise, including a calmer nervous system, a heightened awareness of your body, and an ability to easily prepare yourself for sleep, will be increased by the presence of your salt crystal lamp.

Relaxation exercises cause your blood vessels to dilate, which would theoretically make your body feel warm. Sometimes, however, people in a deep state of relaxation can find themselves shivering with cold. There are different schools of thought about what causes this kind of chill: some people say that being immobile causes you to cool down, while others maintain that the release of mental resistance leaves you feeling "unprotected" and in need of maternal warmth. I leave it up to you to decide the cause and advise you to have a blanket handy in case you do feel the need!

At the beginning of your training, you will do the basic relaxation exercise for fifteen or twenty minutes before you experience deep relaxation. As you progress, you will learn to get into a deeply relaxed state in only a few seconds, just by concentrating on different areas of your body. This is an ability that the salt crystal lamps will reinforce considerably. At that point the prerecording of the basic relaxation technique won't be useful any longer.

Once you have entered the deep relaxation state, which you can recognize by the feeling of pleasant heaviness that takes hold of you, you will be able to address your mental state directly, along with any specific mental or physical problems that are bothering you. In this state of heightened suggestibility, you will be able to "recondition" your mind and body to react differently to the stimuli around you.

I am going to give you a few examples of this by approaching a problem that many of us are familiar with: handling stress effectively. The word *stress* is so trivialized that we no longer know the meaning of it. Most of us assume that it has a negative connotation, though it originally referred to any reaction our bodies might have to stimulus. Stress in its pure form is nothing more than a "healthy shock" designed to get us to accept change.

But stress rarely exists in any kind of "pure" form; as soon as we encounter it, we tend to transform it into a mood. The problem, then, is not so much the stress itself as our reaction to it. We might feel irritable or anxious and may experience physical symptoms such as digestive trouble, headaches, rapid heartbeat, and/or high blood pressure. We don't all react the same way. Some of us are able to surmount stressful situations without difficulty and transform them into assets, while others turn out to be powerless when faced with the slightest difficulty.

Knowing this, we can use relaxation techniques to creatively manage our reactions to stress. We can learn to interpret the alarm signals conveyed by our bodies and use them as well as possible, thereby channeling our emotions into positive change. As importantly, we can learn how to recover from stress reactions so that they don't accumulate into unbridgeable obstacles. As tools for reducing our stress responses, the combination of relaxation techniques and salt crystal lamps is really quite powerful.

To calm your body from an acute or chronic stress reaction, do the basic relaxation exercise described earlier, then listen to the following text. As with the basic relaxation exercise (sometimes called "flying over your body"), you should prerecord this text so it is available when you need it. It will

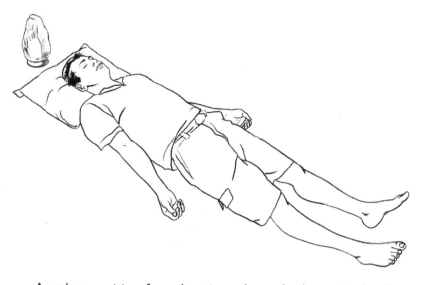

Another position for relaxation where the lamp sits level with the head, acting directly on the Sahasrara chakra (awareness/intelligence)

guide you through the process. Your head will be at the base of a salt crystal lamp. Depending on your degree of sensitivity, you can touch the lamp or not.

Remember that the dots in the text represent spaces during which you should observe silence. Don't rush the language and don't recite mechanically. Give your body as well as your mind the time and chance to adapt to the things being said.

I am becoming aware of my breathing, which is flowing in me freely . . . easily . . . I am listening to the sound of the breath in my body . . . I am being united gradually with my breathing, which is happening in me . . . like a calming wave . . . the more I listen to my breath, the more I am becoming relaxed . . . with each breath, my whole body is letting go . . . is becoming peaceful . . . I am slowly focusing my attention on my solar plexus . . . on the pit of my stomach . . . I am visualizing a ray of sun, gently warming my center . . . this heat is calming me down . . . is making me peaceful . . . it is radiating into my belly with every breath . . . the heat is spreading into my abdomen . . . my thighs . . . all along my legs . . . inside my feet . . . it is going up all along my calves . . . behind my thighs . . . my legs are pleasantly warm . . . I am feeling good . . . the beneficial heat is spreading along my back . . . from the kidneys to my shoulders . . . the current of heat is flowing fluidly in both of my arms . . . inside my chest . . . the warm current is going back to its source in the pit of my stomach . . . my whole body is bathing right now in a sensation of enveloping heat, like in a hot bath . . . only my head remains cool . . . I now know that there is a sensation of well-being within me . . . regenerating me . . . any time I need to, I will remember this moment of peace, which will enable me to find the strength I need to meet all challenges . . .

At this point, you can gradually come back to awareness using the model of the basic relaxation technique.

Right now, I am becoming gradually aware again of the outside world surrounding me . . . every new relaxation process will be deeper and more beneficial . . . I am taking three big breaths . . . I am gently stretching

out my limbs . . . I am moving my toes . . . Radiating
with life, I am opening my eyes.

Initially, you may find it hard to feel the heat and may even feel cold instead. This is not important. Take this sensation as it comes. By practicing, you will soon be able to feel a sensation of heat, and the deep relief that comes along with recovery from a stress response.

Next we will examine a relaxation technique whose main effect is to revitalize the neuro-vegetative system and its functions, producing a feeling of peace and getting rid of the negative consequences of stress. Record the following message beforehand, so you can follow along. Behind your head, the salt crystal lamp should be lit. Our advice is to leave it on for several minutes at the beginning of your recording before you say your first sentences so that you have time to set yourself up as comfortably as possible.

I am now imagining that I am walking in a large
green field . . . the grass that I am treading on is a
beautiful soft green color . . . the wind is shivering
in the trees around me . . . I am seeing the leaves

tremble gently . . . I am immersing myself in this ver-dant countryside . . . this luxuriant nature . . . this chlorophyll . . . everything around me is only growth, balance, harmony . . . green . . . I am breathing the light, regenerating breeze . . . it is inviting me to calm . . . serenity . . . rest . . .

I feel like stretching out on the grass . . . At the foot of the trees, I am clearly seeing moss that is green . . . soft . . . fragrant . . . the grass is receiving my body . . . like a soft bed . . . I am comfortable . . . I am feeling perfectly safe, listening to myself and my sensations . . . the air that I am breathing is an emerald color . . . this green is enveloping me and protecting me from head to toe, like a second skin . . . with each breath, I feel my body bathed in this green color . . . with each exhala-tion, the green is spreading throughout my organism . . . I am feeling completely submerged in the green . . . I am floating pleasantly in the green . . .

After a few minutes of enjoying this healing green imag-ery, you can gradually return to awareness, using the method described above.

The next relaxation technique is designed to help you become aware of your inner potential. It can give you increased dynamism, transform your stress into positive energy, and give you a powerful push toward the future. As you did before, place a salt crystal lamp behind your head. Plan to light it two or three hours before doing your relaxation exercise. If you need to, you can leave it lit for a longer period of time, since salt crystal lamps consume very little electricity and produce very limited heat. Record your phrases in advance, then begin your relaxation exercise.

I am concentrating on the rhythm of my breathing, which is becoming calmer and more regular . . . with each breath, I am relaxing more fully . . . I am letting air enter my nostrils, calmly . . . effortlessly . . . I am mentally following the line of the air as it moves along my respiratory tract . . . into my nostrils . . . the back of my throat . . . into my lungs . . . it is cool when I breathe in and warm when I breathe out . . . I am feeling perfectly calm and perfectly relaxed . . .

I am feeling my body in its total form . . . every cell, every atom of my being, every organ, is fulfilling its role

*perfectly . . . everything in me is unity, harmony, osmosis
. . . I am visualizing myself now at my place of work* (or
within your house or in any other place likely to generate stress for you. So it is up to you to modify this
statement as is appropriate for you.) *. . . I feel perfectly
capable . . . effective . . . responsible . . . this gives me a feeling of strength . . . assurance . . . I see myself accomplishing
my work with a great deal of ease . . . confronting the
difficulties of my professional life with a very powerful
feeling of victory . . . I know that I can make use of every
change . . . of every obstacle . . . I am feeling stronger and
stronger . . . more and more effective . . . stronger and
stronger . . . more and more effective . . . I know now
that I am able to remain calm . . . relaxed . . . when
faced with any situation whatsoever . . . life is getting
easier and easier for me, thanks to the deep relaxation
that I can awaken at any time in my body . . . thanks to
the deep mastery that I exercise over my thoughts . . .*

Come back to awareness of your environment gradually,
using the method I have shown you.

The techniques just described, as well as the methodology inherent in them, form the matrix of many relaxation techniques. While the special relationship between deep relaxation and salt crystal lamps could be the subject of a book all by itself, I believe that the exercises provided will give you enough skill to create personalized relaxation journeys of your own. You can invent specific images of your own with "messages" that suit your particular needs. Just remember that your formulations must be stated in the present indicative tense to be totally effective.

8

SALT CRYSTAL LAMPS AND THE PARANORMAL SCIENCES

Although many of the so-called proofs of paranormal phenomena are only a stack of presumptions, I find it difficult to dismiss paranormal occurrences entirely. Without falling into junk mysticism, I would nevertheless like to state that salt crystal lamps tend to bring forth certain unused abilities of the human brain in natural and beneficial ways.

In this chapter, you will find an alphabetical listing of areas of psychic exploration that seem enhanced by work with salt crystal lamps. I've provided some suggestions of how best to use your lamps in each discipline. This is by no means a complete list; you may be able to add to it after working with a salt crystal lamp of your own.

Chakras

As described in chapter 4, salt crystal lamps are closely connected to three major chakras: Svadhisthana, Manipura, and especially Muladhara, the root chakra. Work with salt crystal lamps can help you open, energize, and stabilize these chakras. Start by choosing the lamp that mirrors as closely as possible the color of the energetic center you would like to work with: red for the root chakra (Muladhara), orange for the Svadhisthana chakra, and yellow for the Manipura chakra. Use either a small or medium-size lamp. Light it up for about two hours, then turn off all other sources of light and put yourself in a lotus position facing the lamp, or a seated position if you prefer.

Empty your mind and get completely absorbed in gazing at your salt crystal lamp for a total length of no more than twenty minutes. You should do this exercise every day for one week.

The major advantage that salt crystal lamps have over other techniques for opening the chakras is that they enable your body to practice at its own pace, so that you avoid the unpleasant side effects that may happen if you open the chakras too quickly. If you wish to energize all of your energetic bodies at the same time, use a large-size lamp.

The lamp acts on the first three chakras—
Muladhara (energy/vitality),
Svadhisthana (sexuality/self-control), and
Manipura (will/power)—
because of its three colors:
red, orange, and yellow.

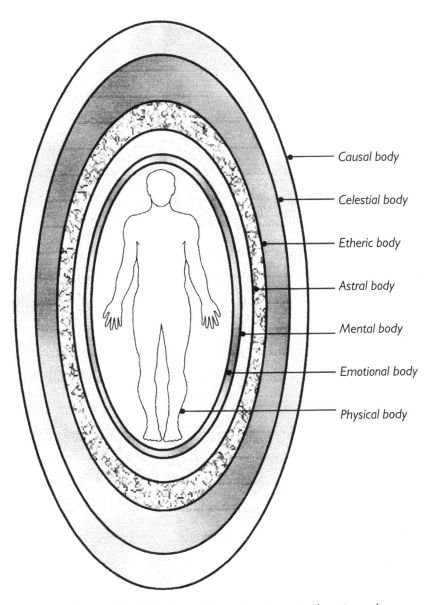

Causal body

Celestial body

Etheric body

Astral body

Mental body

Emotional body

Physical body

Thanks to the diffusion of negative ions in the air and the emission of colors, the lamp strengthens and energizes our energy bodies.

Clairvoyance

Knowing that time is not absolute—even from a scientific point of view—it seems hard to exclude the possibility that we can explore, in our minds, both the past and our potential futures. Nearly anyone you ask can tell at least one or two stories of clairvoyant perceptions that they've experienced. Sometimes such information is so specific that it is hard, even impossible, to attribute it to pure coincidence.

It is possible to enhance your own clairvoyant abilities using salt crystal lamps along with meditation and relaxation techniques. Some people find them even more effective than crystal balls. If you already have a practice that encourages psychic vision (for instance, card reading or palm reading), then simply place a salt lamp on the table where you work. The lamp should be placed to your right and should remain in your visual field. If you are practicing for yourself, don't hesitate to place your forehead on top of the lamp, or both your hands around it, to increase your concentration. You will soon come to realize that you are a great deal more effective, receiving visual and auditory flashes of a rare quality thanks to the contribution of the lamp.

Another major application in the area of clairvoyance consists of strengthening the objects that you use for support in your readings—such as tarot cards, a pendulum, or a crystal ball. Simply place these things at the base of a lighted salt crystal lamp for three whole days. This will make them more efficient.

Contact Objects

In pursuing any kind of paranormal work, we sometimes have a need to return very quickly to our everyday world, to make a break between two levels of reality that are fundamentally different in their essence. This may happen if we find ourselves confronted with negative forces that we are unable to control successfully, or simply if we are tired or feel hurried. From a state close to sleepwalking, it is not easy to make this return trip without side effects, which can include persistent feelings of unreality, depression, rapid heartbeat, and temporary but unpleasant hypo- or hyperthermia, among other things.

In these circumstances it is tremendously helpful to have a *contact object* whose role is to bring us back to reality through its material presence. Such an object should be relatively massive or at least dense, slightly rough but not sharp-edged, and its touch should bring up immediate physical sensations. Salt crystal lamps make ideal contact objects. The principle is simple but effective: Always keep one close at hand, and in case of panic, seize it firmly. This will instantaneously bring you back to a feeling of reality and will soothe any unpleasant sensations. The warm, elemental touch of the salt crystal, along with its soft light and the rich harmony of colors, will calm your anxieties and provide a smooth "re-entry" into your everyday world.

Crystal Programming

Crystal programming is a way of asking a crystal to clarify and amplify your intentions as you work with it. There are many methods for achieving this "programming," which is actually more like making a contract than imposing your will on the stone. However, numerous experiments done with specialists in the field have proved that any such programming is achieved more quickly, and with longer-lasting results, when you do it with your hand outstretched above a salt crystal lamp. When you bring your healing crystal into the energy field of a salt crystal lamp, the two minerals will work together for your greater well-being. This effect becomes even more dramatic when you use a lamp whose color tends toward a dark orange but doesn't extend into the red color zones.

Practitioners of crystal programming know that between

each new programmed goal, a crystal must be "de-saturated"—usually by plunging it into a basin of water salted with rock salt. However, a large-size salt crystal lamp can replace this soaking operation. Just place your crystal at the foot of the lamp, which should remain lit for one whole night.

All you have to do is place stones or a rock crystal near the salt lamp for them to be purified and recharged.

Dowsing

The presence of a salt crystal lamp during dowsing work—even a small-size one—considerably increases its effectiveness. This improvement is noticed even among beginners, whom it shelters from many initial mistakes. To make use

A salt lamp will help the dowser concentrate
better and get clear results.

of this benefit, light a salt crystal lamp at least two hours before going to work. The lamp can be near you, or placed anywhere in the room where you work. The objects or photos you wish to test will be placed at its base—the same way as a plan for doing research. If you use a pendulum as an instrument, you should suspend it above the salt lamp when you ask your questions.

To dowse under ideal conditions, you will actually have two salt lamps, one at each end of the table on which you will be doing your research, whatever type of work that may be. Such an arrangement enables you to obtain exceptional results.

Feng Shui

We have already seen how salt crystal lamps skillfully combine each of the elements in the Chinese tradition: Water through their origin, Wood through the wooden base, Fire through their colors, Earth where salt rests in hidden deposits, and Metal through the minerals that comprise and enrich the rock salt. Placed in any zone of your home that corresponds to a specific realm of your life, a salt crystal lamp will exert a strongly positive influence. However, to effectively practice feng shui using salt crystal lamps, it is essential to have several different sizes and shades that will be adapted more to fill specific needs. For more details, see chapter 6, which is dedicated to this subject.

Healing

There are countless techniques of healing, all of which rely on a practitioner's ability to recognize and reorganize energetic disturbances. Some styles such as massage, Rolfing, and acupuncture use hands-on methods, while others, such as energy healing, keep the practitioner's hands a few inches above a client's body.

For healers, the salt lamp will become the indispensable tool for "cleaning" and recharging yourself after laying on your hands.

Salt crystal lamps are terrific assets in any healing practice. First of all, they enhance the ability of the body and mind to relax, which are conditions needed for practicing any healing technique well. Second, salt lamps will recharge the practitioner, helping her to avoid being destabilized by the illnesses of those whose healing process she is accelerating. It is a good idea, for example, to put your hands directly on the lamp before and after a session. This will help cleanse and recharge your energy body as well as your hands. Use a large-size lamp in your treatment room, and light it up an hour before you begin your session.

Magic

Magic in modern times has become synonymous with superstition and is considered impossible and false. Yet we forget that the word *magic* has the same origin as *major* and once referred to something basic, essential, and vital. Magic was the Major Art, because it included all the others. (Witchcraft, a type of magic, was simply the discipline of casting spells.) But just because the word and the concept are out of fashion doesn't mean that the phenomena do not exist in concrete reality.

I can tell you that many skeptics I know have practiced

specific rituals out of pure curiosity and have had a few surprises. At its most basic level (and there are several levels beyond this), magic is a conscious projection of our will toward a goal. It is our volitional strength, carried into incandescence and passed through energetic levels, that cause events to be modified.

What relationship does this have with salt crystal lamps? By relaxing the body and the mind, salt crystal lamps help us to modify our level of awareness and our brain waves. Through the richness of their colors (directly perceived by our cerebral cortex), their subtle olfactory emanations, and their filtered light, salt crystal lamps help us achieve the deeply relaxed and focused awareness that is necessary for any kind of ritual.

Another advantage of using salt crystal lamps during magic work is that they help you avoid falling into extremes and becoming destabilized by negative forces. Such forces, whether they come from envious attacks by others or the shameful thoughts that you hide from yourself, can be effectively neutralized by the power of salt. We know that salt has traditionally been used to keep the Devil away; if you replace the word *devil* with a more modern notion like *harmful waves, negative thoughts,* or attitudes of hatred and

During your meditation sessions, the salt lamp will protect you from psychic attacks, creating a protective bubble around you.

destruction, you will perhaps understand the nature of this phenomenon a little better.

To use a salt crystal lamp for magical purposes, it should be situated at eye level, so it can be a focal point for your concentration. Use a large-size lamp when possible, and avoid ones with colors that are too red.

Meditation

There are many different kinds of meditation, but all of them are enhanced by the use of salt crystal lamps. In general, you can divide meditation practices into two kinds: passive and active. In passive meditation, you can simply stare at a salt crystal lamp for several minutes a day, without any other kind of lighting, either in a lotus position if you master it, or seated across from it. You might try what is called "emptying your mind" and concentrating just on this one focal point. Let the thoughts that come to you pass through, without trying to examine them or get rid of them. Don't even try to find any kind of significance or coherence in them, just let them go, like ripples that disappear from a pond.

Active meditation consists of concentrating on specific thoughts. These might be in the form of words, sounds, or images. This kind of meditation will help you evolve. However, it requires a good knowledge of symbolism and perfect mastery of visualization.

Whatever kind of meditation you practice, the salt crystal lamp will act on you like a mental purge, emptying thoughts from you that harm your evolution or balance. These thoughts may arise within you in different ways on subsequent days and probably through your dreams, allowing you to settle some internal conflicts.

Planetary Consciousness

Although planetary consciousness is one of the oldest concepts we have, it is attracting new interest today as part of modern spirituality movements. Simply put, planetary consciousness is a deep feeling of belonging and interconnection among all living beings inhabiting our planet. From the moment we become aware of this interconnection, we cease to feel isolated, but instead recognize ourselves as an integral part of a vast whole to which we try to bring our harmonious contribution.

It is actually hard to persist in pathological behaviors and actions when we have such a feeling of being connected to the rest of the universe. I myself have noted that continued use of salt crystal lamps seems to cultivate this wider awareness, whether or not it was consciously sought. Perhaps it is a natural evolution that we human beings are working toward. In any case, don't be afraid of it, for you will draw huge benefits from your improved relationship with the rest of the planet. On spiritual as well as material levels, you will notice wonderful changes, simply because the way you act will no longer be the same.

Positive Thinking

By contributing to better mental, physical, and spiritual balance, regular use of salt crystal lamps greatly increases your ability to think positively. Over time it may even change the way you perceive and understand the world, awakening you to the reality of abundance. Welcome to the world of creative optimism!

Protection

Just as salt protects and preserves food, principles of magical analogy suggest that it also protects the soul and provides shelter to those who call upon it from occult attacks of all kinds. Be assured that ancient practitioners of magic tested their materials for a long time before deciding that a tool was spiritually active. That was the case with rock salt and salt crystal lamps. While our explanations today may revolve around electromagnetic fields and negative ions, we still maintain the principle that salt crystal shields your home and those inside it from all forms of aggression.

To activate the protective powers of your salt crystal lamp, it's a good idea to establish "contact" with it. Touch your lamp, feel its contours with your fingers. Maintain respect and admiration—not the kind you have for a god, but the kind you feel toward a work tool that functions extremely well. Think about all the ways salt has demonstrated its protective abilities throughout the millennia.

You can also generate protection for other people by placing photos of them at the foot of a medium- to large-size salt crystal lamp, which should then remain lit for two whole days. Even after this time, you will be able to touch the lamp without getting burned.

You should position photos under the wooden base of a medium- to large-size lamp.

After the two days have elapsed, arrange your photos nearby, turn off the lamp, and inscribe the names of the people you wish to call protection for on small individual pieces of paper. Fold your pieces, take the bulb out of the lamp and arrange the papers in the hollow part of your rock salt block. Leave them like that for two days, then pick them up and place the still-folded papers in your wallet. With this practice, you will be continuing to call in protection for people as long as you are keeping their names in your thoughts and among your belongings.

Purification

Rock salt can be used for spiritual purification just like it is for protection. This idea is also based on the fact of salt's antibacterial and antiseptic qualities. Since salt can prevent the decay of food, why wouldn't it also cleanse our spirits?

In fact, I believe that daily meditation in front of a salt crystal lamp does produce a sort of cleansing of our mental state—especially when that lamp is the only lighting in the room. By a "cleansing" of our mental state I mean that in time we will tend more often to do the right thing at the right time, and our thinking will become clearer, more lucid, more attentive, and more vigilant. We will be heading little by little toward a kind of internal peace, which will be felt in our relationships with others, and our minds will be more open to the world around us. These effects may be due to the lamps' joint actions of negative ionization, chromotherapeutic effects, and the development of the chakras.

Radionics

Radionics is a method of influencing events from a distance. It goes well beyond active dowsing, which mainly relies on the use of a pendulum. Radionics practitioners may use graphic tools, geometry, even electronics to create powerful energy circuits. Such work *does* have consequences, and not all of them are positive. Like magic, radionics demands great self-control and self-awareness, and it isn't any less dangerous for people who simply don't know what they're getting into.

For those who wish to practice radionics or who already practice it, know that salt lamps are an indispensable asset. Your salt block will take its place above your device and can limit how far off course it goes. It will also prevent you from venturing into realms that are too dangerous. In this context, the salt lamp establishes what could be called a vibratory regulation, through which it provides balance and a harmonious orientation of your sensibility and will.

This pyramidal shape achieved by using three salt lamps will form a real shield, a protection against harmful waves.

Ideally, you will arrange three salt lamps in a triangle: the strong symbolism of this geometric shape will add its protective power to the strength of the salt crystal lamps. Put two medium-size lamps on the sides and one small lamp tending toward a yellow color at the apex. In this way you will be perfectly surrounded and sheltered from any unpleasant surprises.

Reiki

The idea of a universal life force that is present in all forms of life is common to a large number of traditions throughout the world. For Melanesians, it is *mana*—from which we get our word *manager.* But this concept is found in ancient civilizations from the Indians of North America to the Siberian

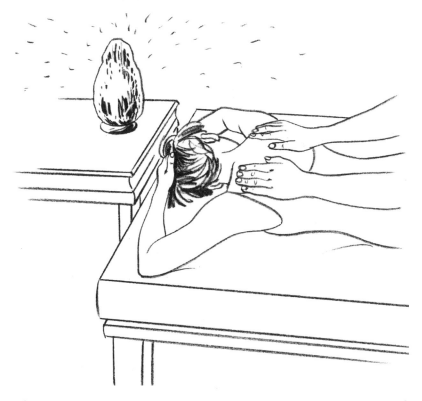

During a Reiki session, a salt lamp will create an atmosphere of calm and harmony. The practitioner and the patient will feel energized and recharged.

Yakutes, and from South America to Africa and Asia. The Asian version of this life force is *chi,* and in that tradition, this force circulates freely across everything and does not get attached.

Our vitality and balance depend on the free circulation of chi, as does our relationship to the material world, including our finances. If we are sick, or constantly in the red monetarily, if our love life turns out catastrophically, it is because our energy is blocked at one level or another. By unblocking such bolts, and thereby allowing chi to flow freely once again in all areas of our lives, we can move toward a richer, more harmonious existence on all levels.

A growing number of Reiki practitioners are turning to salt crystal lamps, having noticed that their effects combine harmoniously with the transmission of the Reiki and help to establish a climate of absolute confidence between the practitioner and the person being treated.

Reincarnation

Regression into past lives can help us to understand and resolve persistent patterns of behavior and thought. One technique for achieving such regressions is known as "rebirthing." Rebirthing experiences can be quite powerful, and also quite dramatic; they are not necessarily easy or innocuous. Instead, they can be quite complicated and can bring up unexpected physical reactions. I should point out that one of the methods often used to accomplish such a journey into the core requires us to over-oxygenate our bodies, which is not necessarily risk-free. It is advisable to do this under the direction of an experienced practitioner who is used to dealing with the kinds of phenomena that occur during rebirthing sessions.

Practitioners who have used salt crystal lamps during rebirthing sessions have widely confirmed that the lamps are enormously helpful in the process. One important benefit is that lamps limit the problems that can occur from over-oxygenation. Another is that, with a salt lamp in the room, rebirthing clients reach deep states of awareness more quickly and often go further back into the past, recalling essential moments of their past lives from the very first session. Last of all, according to the clients themselves, the return to reality is less painful, more serene, and accomplished more easily in the presence of a salt crystal lamp.

For assistance in rebirthing and regression work, a lamp should be placed behind the head of the person who is going into regression, closer or farther according to what the client wishes. It seems that better results are obtained on a glass table—probably because, like rock salt, they are a fusion of water and mineral elements.

Relaxation Techniques

In chapter 7, we saw the many benefits that a salt crystal lamp can bring to a relaxation process. In general, a lamp will multiply the effects of your relaxation practice. Some practitioners also note that they achieve even deeper states of relaxation when they physically touch the lamp before they begin the practice.

Shape Waves

The use of geometric shapes to concentrate energy in specific ways goes back to earliest antiquity. Some familiar examples of this use of form are Stonehenge, sacred architecture including the great cathedrals of Europe, magical squares, the Egyptian pyramids, and the protective value given to the circle.

Students of spiritual geometry emphasize the existing relationship between certain geometric volumes and the physical effects they have on life-forms placed inside or around them. Used this way, shapes are thought to positively affect plant growth, the aging of wine, rates of scar formation, insomnia, migraine headaches, and many other developments. Practitioners of the psychic arts also note that particular shape waves can increase one's skills at telepathy, clairvoyance, and magic as well. These latter are of course the hardest to measure.

A researcher named André Bovis explored some of the principles of sacred geometry at the beginning of the twentieth century. He was interested in the fact that animals that had wandered into the Great Pyramid of Cheops were found mummified, in the absence of any human intervention. He had the idea of reproducing this pyramid to scale and to try some experiments, whose results astounded him. Similar studies were carried out in the 1950s by a Czech scientist, Karel Drbal. His experiments were revealed to the general public in the 1970s, before they disappeared behind the Iron Curtain.

For modern people studying the effects of form on matter, the presence of salt crystal lamps is said to greatly increase the results of any experiment. To test this benefit, place a medium-size lamp at the magnetic north pole of your geometric form.

As for the "dream machine" aspect of pyramids and

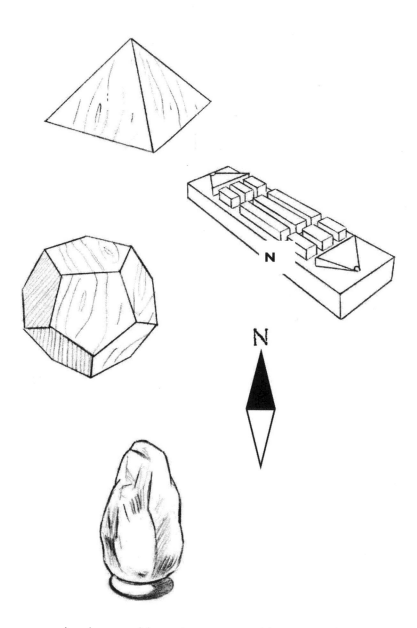

A salt crystal lamp increases and improves the
emissions from shape wave devices.

dodecahedrons, these results are also much faster and more convincing with a salt crystal lamp by your side than with standard ritual methods alone. The lamps no doubt increase our volitional energy as well as our ability to let go.

Spells

First of all, you should be aware that most spells do not come from magical practices. On the contrary, we are more often confronted with self-induced spells, or sometimes telepathic ones, than with spells deriving from hate-oriented magic. Self-induced spells are cast when we stigmatize a failure and focus on it so much that we end up making it inescapable; a new causality gets put in place inadvertently. In other words, a moment arrives where even if we had a conscious will to succeed, our subconscious would have such control over us that we would condemn ourselves to fail.

Telepathic spells come from the way that other people sometimes transmit negative programming or negative expectations about us. These negative ideas can influence us if we are unknowingly receptive following a state of weakness.

Both of the examples above are "minor" spells, which can easily be eradicated if we take charge of ourselves and our thoughts. From a rational point of view, you could compare them with purely psychological phenomena. Whatever the case, outside help is often needed to pull yourself out of such diabolical patterns. Salt crystal lamps are an ideal tool in this case. Through their negative ions and their relaxing qualities, they bring us the strength and distance necessary for seeing ourselves and others clearly.

To benefit from a salt lamp's ability to help clarify your view, practice the basic relaxation technique with your head oriented toward magnetic north, and the lamp right behind you.

After a couple of sessions, you will regain your energy and your ability to act effectively. You will find yourself better able to chase away the gloomy ideas that sit at the deepest levels of your being, and in so doing will take your life back

Orientation toward magnetic north will protect you
from telepathic waves during relaxation sessions.

into your own hands. In the case of a serious spell, these methods might not be enough to completely remove it, but you will get an obvious feeling of well-being and can use the interlude of peace and serenity to consider your next steps.

Spiritualism

The practice of invoking the dead has been around for countless centuries. Since this occult art requires an open passage between two realms of existence, it can leave the practitioner and all those present vulnerable to many energies that are not necessarily beneficial. A spiritualist medium could in fact find herself confronted by powers for which her will alone is insufficient to assure absolute control, or she might be visited by spirits that she had not consciously called upon.

Whether one uses automatic writing, a Ouija board, or a séance table, a reliable method of protection is necessary to ensure the safety of those present. Salt crystal lamps serve as powerful allies in this endeavor; they essentially draw good spirits toward the practitioners, attracting entities who are animated by good intentions while repelling all others.

For proper protection, your lamp should be set up and lit

at least three hours before the beginning of the session. You should place it in the center of your table, above any other tools you need. Ideally, you would use three lamps in the pattern of a triangle surrounding your working area: a small lamp at the top of your table and two medium-size lamps at the sides forming the base of the triangle. If you have two lamps, place them at the two ends of the table. Whatever the spiritualist methodology you use, your salt crystal lamps will have a double function: first of all, to purify the atmosphere and thereby protect you; second to serve as a contact object so that you can come back to normality quickly in case of problems, which should, in any case, be limited by the presence of the lamps.

Spirituality

By spirituality, I don't mean an exclusive mystical vision or the search for paranormal phenomena. Rather, I'm referring to a general notion of a path to awakening—the search for understanding of the true nature of things. Decades ago, Mircea Eliade pointed out that spirituality was not a fixed moment in human history but a fundamental need of human beings. We seek what is real beyond mere appearances, to grasp the workings of creation and not run away from or resist the truth. In this sense, salt crystal lamps exert an undeniable influence on our evolution.

Salt lamps open up the gates of perception in us. This is true whether we simply have them in a room where we sleep, work, or play, or whether we work actively with them via meditation. In either case, they prompt us to recognize deeper levels of connection to all of creation. As discussed throughout this book, salt crystal lamps have a remarkable ability to remind us of our true nature. They serve as a kind of portal to a realm of deeper understanding.

Telepathy

All molecules, through their atoms—and especially in their electrons—are loaded with information. These atoms "communicate" among themselves with the result that the universe is a backdrop for the perpetual exchange of informed energies. One way to understand telepathy is as a form of communication with—and via—these energies.

Salt crystal lamps are true energetic sponges, and they can help you improve your telepathic skills if you work with them regularly. Any energies that you seek to transmit or receive will be transformed, purified, and multiplied by the rock salt before they are sent back to you, or to a partner

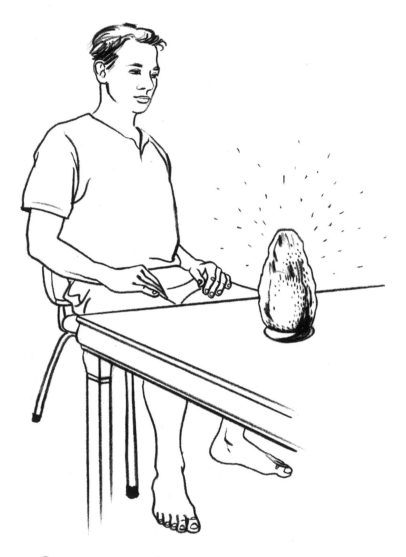

Concentrating on the salt lamp's light in a relatively
dark room will enhance your telepathic skills.

you are working with. Practicing telepathy in a room where a salt crystal lamp is the only source of lighting will quickly strike you as powerful. You should always place it facing you, and for optimal results you should position the lamp at eye level, for it will be a focal point of a rare intensity.

Visualization

In the chapter on relaxation techniques (see page 67), I mentioned that a salt crystal lamp in a room guarantees good concentration. You should light it up a few hours beforehand. Your room will then seem lighter, purified. Turn off the central light and concentrate your attention on the lamp. After a few days of passive meditation, you can go on to visualization, and you will notice that the latter is accomplished in an amazingly fluid way, whatever your degree of experience.

Another technique consists of setting up a lamp behind you, slightly off-center and toward the right, so that it still remains in your visual field. Then set up a big mirror across from you and concentrate your attention on the reflection of your salt lamp. For visualization as for clairvoyance, this method produces truly exceptional results.

9

THE POWER OF PHOSPHENES

It would seem strange to us in concluding this book not to mention the phenomenon of phosphenes. Phosphenes are colored circles that appear on the retina when no light is present. These images can be directly induced by mechanical, electrical, or magnetic stimulation. Most of us have learned about this phenomenon through spontaneous experiment, for example, by pressing on our eyelids or staring at candles or a fireplace. They will often appear after you stare for several minutes at a 60-watt lamp or any other type of light. Phosphenes are pretty to look at and can feel like internal fireworks or a personal kaleidoscope, but their significance extends way beyond this idle interest.

A French doctor named Francis Lefébure devoted a good part of his life to studying phosphenes and their relationship to our thoughts and abilities. In his books, seminars, and experiments, Lefébure demonstrated the influence of phosphenes on memory and will and also on parapsychic phenomena. (He conducted similar experiments on phenomena that occur to our senses of hearing and taste, but it is the visual aspects that most concern us here.)

By studying cases of pronounced mediumship, Lefébure noticed that a medium's skills often emerged after he or she had seen vivid phosphenes. He observed that in shamanic cultures around the world there is often a moment when an initiate must remain alone in the dark, meditating, after having stared at a candle for a long time. It is only after that, once he has acquired strength and a capacity for new thinking, that an initiate can pursue his path, the quest of his internal light.

Lefébure wondered if phosphenes might play a role in spiritual development, so he began to generate them voluntarily and experiment with them. He pioneered a technique of visualizing images or phrases within the phosphene's circle, which he called "phosphenic mixing." He taught that the practice of phosphenic mixing on a regular basis would lead to improved memory and concentration, the development of psychic skills, and a greater ability to manifest ideals that were visualized in this way.

Mixing a thought with a phosphene strengthens its coherence and helps to engender its fulfillment, if only by programming the unconscious, which will push us toward the actions needed for accomplishment.

Salt crystal lamps are perfect tools for generating phosphenes. They don't have the aggressive character of most electric lights, and they avoid the ritual aspect of candles, which can lend themselves too easily to mystical extremes we would not know how to control. In addition, you can stare at a salt crystal lamp for a long time (though at a respectable distance), without there being a risk to your optic nerves. The phosphenes you generate this way will last longer than those generated by other methods, which is a considerable asset. Your thoughts will be able to imprint within the phosphene for a longer period of time.

To practice phosphene mixing, first do a modified basic relaxation exercise—in a sitting position. Your lamp should be placed in front of you on a piece of furniture that is at eye level. Stare at it for a few moments. When you have found an image, phrase, symbol, or key word that you would like to energize, go ahead and create a phosphene by turning your head away from the lamp and closing your eyes. At the moment a phosphene appears, visualize in the center of the colored circle a representation of your goal.

Does the phosphene disappear before it appears again? Does it follow the movements of your thoughts? Try to relax and let your thoughts go. Focus on the image. Try to work on this regularly as much as possible, at a time you have set up in advance. For instance, you can practice every night before going to bed, until your wish is fulfilled. This regularity will enable you to develop your visualization skills and to get results that are more and more convincing each time.

In the process of helping you achieve specific goals, phosphenic mixing will also increase your general well-being. By deepening your initial state of relaxation—which constitutes a kind of "flight path"—the phosphenic phenomenon will enable you to expand your awareness. In fact, what's happening here is a "phosphenic mixing" of a special type; in this case, the phosphene does not crystallize only a thought, but an entire state of being. You will feel more present, living each moment fully. You will also develop a certain kind of openness, which will make you aware of subtle energies you may not have noticed before.

Practicing phosphenes is especially well-adapted to modern man's way of life, since it only takes a couple of minutes a day. In addition to the benefits described above, it will help you develop or improve faculties that have been lying fallow until now. All parapsychological exercises done after a phosphenism session will have special power—especially clairvoyant exercises. You may even discover an ability to have premonitory dreams.

Phosphenes also facilitate memorization. You will easily retain a lesson learned at the moment the phosphenes appeared, a fact that has been taken into account by several schools in Quebec and on the African continent. In the area of self-programming and self-hypnosis, phosphenic mixing also does wonders, strengthening the will and powers of memorization in sometimes phenomenal proportions. Used in this way, practicing phosphenism increases one's will considerably and can even intervene in breaking an addiction, especially to tobacco.

I hope you can see that phosphenism is a fantastic tool for personal fulfillment of almost any variety you can imagine. By using your salt crystal lamp to generate this fascinating phenomenon, you will be connecting your personal goals with the power and beauty of the oceans, our Earth, and all of humanity.

CONCLUSION

I hope this book has helped you get an idea of how vital an asset salt crystal lamps can be in stimulating your health and well-being. Although we understand the lamps' physiological actions relatively well, their impact on energetic levels is still quite mysterious to us. Resolving this mystery is difficult because further exploration is bound up in a profound ideological divide. Two "camps"—one materialist, the other mystical—are both convinced of the validity of their convictions and the falsity of the other side's theories. To me, both are absurd. Denying the existence of other levels of reality and modified states of awareness makes as little sense as wanting to codify such states of awareness without real research.

If only the resources of these two camps could be brought together without ideological blinders, our knowledge of the benefits of salt crystal lamps would move forward with giant steps. Some scientists are trying to establish a healthy relationship between traditional sciences and modern science, but these pioneers are often rejected by their peers. The paths forged by the physicists Fritjof Capra and Costa de Beauregard have not been much followed.

In his book *Supernature: A Natural History of the Supernatural,* botanist and zoologist Lyall Watson suggests that what we have been calling "supernatural" doesn't exist because everything belongs to nature, even if we don't have an immediate explanation for it. For example, he notes that since the moon has an influence on the tides, and since human beings are made up of 70 percent water, how can we *not* assume that the nocturnal star would have an impact on the human body and brain?

This thought seems even more relevant to us in the context of a study done by the French scientist René Quinton in the beginning of the twentieth century. Quinton noted that our bodies are not only made up of 70 percent water, but our internal seas are in other ways very similar to the oceanic environment. Our bodies in fact contain 9 percent salt, over half of which is found in the very heart of our cells. Our blood has the same rate of salinity. Moreover, we contain mineral salts that are similar to those in the marine environment: sodium, potassium, calcium, magnesium. This makes it easier to understand the resonance that exists between salt crystal lamps and our anatomy.

René Quinton was able to prove the validity of his theories by doing cruel but convincing experiments on animals. Draining most of a dog's blood, he injected the animal with salt water modified to match the body's saline proportion. The result was astonishing: the animal got back on its feet very quickly and reconstituted its initial blood formula in less than a week's time. Afterward, Quinton cured several scrawny animals and many children through this formula, obtaining conclusive results every time.

We have seen that salt crystal lamps create negative ionization of the atmosphere, which greatly benefits the human body. But that's not all: when your lamp is lit, it diffuses microparticles of salt. In other words, it nourishes you with mineral salts, those well-known "trace elements." While we know that salt is harmful to us in large quantities, it is a little-known fact that in microdoses, the effect is exactly the opposite. Microparticles of salt energize our internal organs, helping blood to flow and our digestive and nervous systems to function smoothly.

The human body interacts with—and is influenced by—its ambient environment. It becomes obvious to those of us who use salt crystal lamps regularly, especially if this use includes physical contact, that a kind of relationship develops between the lamp and you, an immediate connection that goes well beyond a simple molecular exchange.

Much of the human brain is still terra incognita for us, and we know that we use only a small portion of its enormous potential. Do our brain cells change when we interact regularly with salt crystal lamps? We don't know. We do know that having a salt crystal block at hand allows us to cross the barriers of time and enter into a metaphysical dimension. Rock salt blocks, which came out of the ocean and were transmuted by the earth to the point of becoming an integral part of it, are our connection to a prehumanity that it is extremely hard for us to imagine.

Some authors even affirm that a gift of rock salt will lighten your karmic debt. I do not think that this is possible. The notion of freeing oneself from a karmic debt without ever becoming aware of that debt comes across as false and against the very definition of karma. Karma is a law of causality that concerns past lives and that can also be applied perfectly to our present existence. It is only by becoming aware of the nature of our mistakes, and by changing our orientation, that we can modify our future by freeing ourselves from ingrained patterns of behavior.

Whatever the case, salt crystal lamps excite the imagination a great deal through the fantastic journey they have made to reach us. Beyond their undeniable effects on our physical and psychic selves, it would seem that they set up another field of coherence in which everything becomes possible. Freeing the spirit from the constraints that a stressful way of life imposes, they enable us to go further, to the deepest part of ourselves.

In the same way that a sick body has a hard time accomplishing things and finds itself well below the performance level it could accomplish in a state of full health, an oppressed spirit struggles to find the paths of harmony and cannot express the essence of its "salt." A simple and beautiful remedy for this kind of spiritual illness can be found in salt crystal lamps. Whether this is through the simple fact of negative ionization or some other mechanism, they are powerful agents of change.

The saturation of our air with positive ions seriously handicaps our powers of thought and our ability to reach our human potential. Change this one simple thing, and a profound change will take place in you as you become free of constraints you were previously aware of in only a limited way. By reestablishing balance, salt crystal lamps deeply influence our metaphysical and metapsychic abilities. The dormant parts of our brains, relieved of everything that was crippling them, can finally acquire their true dimensions.

Each of us has gifts of perception that are called "paranormal" but which are in fact more about using our five senses well than about the discovery of a "sixth" sense. Besides having an education that pushes us toward materialism, this more complete expression of ourselves is too often hampered by the negative influence of the outside environment. By eliminating obstacles, we are able once again to progress on the path of the overconscious.

Acting in close collaboration with medicine, salt crystal lamps will enhance the regeneration of your cells and will accelerate the self-healing process considerably. It should be noted that salt crystal lamps can have extremely diversified effects—not just according to their colors, shapes, and sizes but also according to the specific outlook and metabolism of the individuals using them. Nevertheless, the diverse range of effects will all be extremely positive, both for the body and for the mind. Although they have an obvious impact on our body, salt crystal lamps should not be confused with any kind of medication and should in no way be substituted for an appropriate medical treatment.

There's no doubt we have not finished discovering the unbelievable potential of salt crystal lamps. I won't go on and on praising their qualities but will leave readers with the enormous pleasure of discovering these qualities themselves.

INDEX

BOOKS OF RELATED INTEREST

Shungite
Protection, Healing, and Detoxification
by Regina Martino

Energy Medicine Technologies
Ozone Healing, Microcrystals,
Frequency Therapy, and the Future of Health
Edited by Finley Eversole, Ph.D.

The Honey Prescription
The Amazing Power of Honey as Medicine
by Nathaniel Altman

Optimal Detox
How to Cleanse Your Body of Colloidal and Crystalline Toxins
by Christopher Vasey, N.D.

The Oxygen Prescription
The Miracle of Oxidative Therapies
by Nathaniel Altman

The Aura-Soma Sourcebook
Color Therapy for the Soul
by Mike Booth with Carol McKnight

Vibrational Medicine
The #1 Handbook of Subtle-Energy Therapies
by Richard Gerber, M.D.

The Metaphysical Book of Gems and Crystals
by Florence Mégemont

Inner Traditions • Bear & Company
P.O. Box 388
Rochester, VT 05767
1-800-246-8648
www.InnerTraditions.com

Or contact your local bookseller